THE ART OF THE TURNAROUND

THE ART OF

THE TURNAROUND

CREATING AND

MAINTAINING HEALTHY

ARTS ORGANIZATIONS

MICHAEL M. KAISER

BRANDEIS UNIVERSITY PRESS

Waltham, Massachusetts

Published by

University Press of New England

Hanover & London

BRANDEIS UNIVERSITY PRESS
Published by
University Press of New England
One Court Street, Lebanon, NH 03766
www.upne.com
© 2008 by Brandeis University Press
Printed in the United States of America
5 4 3 2 1

Library of Congress Cataloging-in-Publication Data
Kaiser, Michael M.
The art of the turnaround : creating and maintaining
healthy arts organizations / Michael M. Kaiser.
p.   cm.
Includes index.
ISBN 978–1–58465–735–4 (cloth : alk. paper)
1. Performing arts—Management. 2. Kaiser, Michael M. I. Title.
PN1584.K24   2008
791'.068—dc22   2008014479

University Press of New England is a member of the Green Press Initiative.
The paper used in this book meets their minimum requirement for recycled paper.

CONTENTS

ACKNOWLEDGMENTS

This book may make it seem as if I accomplished every turnaround by myself. The truth is I have had incredibly able support from too many people to mention. I would be remiss if I did not recognize those staff members who were most involved in my work: Alicia Adams, Kevin Amey, Darrell Ayers, Mickey Berra, Paul Carlson, Donya Corry, Tiki Davies, Eleanor Goldwin, Dan Hagerty, Calvin Hunt, Peter Katona, Jane Kaufman, Maria Kersten, David Kitto, David Lansky, Sharon Luckman, Marie Mattson, Chris Millard, Rhoda Oster, Sathi Pillai, Bob Pontarelli, Lynne Pratt, Garth Ross, Anthony Russell-Roberts, Chris Samms, John Seekings, Rita Shapiro, Rick Shaw, Ann Stock, Lynn Thommen, Max Woodward. These remarkable people, literally hundreds of Board members, and thousands of artists have been the true turnaround kings and queens, princes and princesses, dukes and duchesses. It was not always fun, but any fun there was resulted from their camaraderie and good fellowship.

There is one person who has been with me, on and off, for my entire arts career. The careful reader will see Claudette Donlon mentioned several times—at the Kansas City Ballet, at American Ballet Theatre, and at the Kennedy Center. Claudette has always been willing to play bad cop to my good cop. I would have accomplished nothing without her and she knows it. Now it is time for others to know this as well.

M.M.K.

INTRODUCTION

My father wanted me to be a dentist because he said I would always be in demand. I have a different suggestion for those seeking a secure profession: make a career of turning around troubled performing arts organizations. In my twenty-plus-year career, I have found no shortage of job opportunities.

So many arts organizations find themselves in difficulty because the "industry" has built-in economic problems.

The primary and underlying problem of the performing arts is that it is very difficult to improve productivity. While other industries cover the cost of inflation by increasing worker productivity through the use of computers, new technologies, and better systems, these approaches are not available in the arts. There are the same number of performers in *Hamlet* as when Shakespeare wrote it centuries ago and the same number of musicians in the New York Philharmonic as when Tchaikovsky conducted it more than one hundred years ago. Costs go up, but we cannot reduce the labor content.

This challenge is compounded by a limitation on ticket sales. Once we select a theater, our real income is bounded. We only have so many seats to sell for a given performance. Once we sell out our theater, we have no ability to increase earned revenue. Where other industries can expand markets, in our peculiar industry we cannot.

I remember taking the Alvin Ailey American Dance Theater to perform at the Herod Atticus, a beautiful Roman amphitheater built into the base of the Acropolis in Athens, Greece. The audience sat on stone bleachers with the Acropolis lit up by moonlight just behind. It was a magical site and my dancers were thrilled to be there. I simply stood on stage and remarked that the number of seats had not increased in two thousand years!

With limited productivity improvement and no ability to expand ticket sales the performing arts industry faces a severe gap between earnings and expenses. And this gap continues to widen as expenses rise and revenue is bounded. The four major approaches to filling this gap are all fraught with difficulty.

Most organizations have tried to fill the "income gap" by raising ticket prices. This has resulted in substantial loss of audience for many arts organizations. Much of our audience is very price sensitive, and there are so many substitute forms of entertainment, especially with the advent of Internet technology that puts entertainment in the home at almost no cost. The price of opera tickets has risen so fast that one can now buy an entire computer for the cost of two tickets to major opera houses around the world.

As we lose our audiences, there are many cries that the arts have become irrelevant. I do not believe that is the case. Simply look at the Fall for Dance series at City Center in New York, the new pricing structure for the Pittsburgh Symphony, or programs for new audiences at the Royal Opera House, and you will see huge interest in serious performing arts at reasonable prices.

Pricing in a reasonable manner typically demands the second gap-filling technique: raising contribution levels from private or public sources. But the competition for these funds has grown increasingly intense. While one or a few people traditionally served as angels for a given organization it now takes hundreds and thousands of donors. (The Kennedy Center now has thirty thousand contributors on an annual basis, a requirement to balance our books.) This search for new donors places arts organizations in direct competition with each other; it favors the stronger, more accessible organizations particularly in those countries without well-developed cultures of philanthropy.

As a result of the difficulty wooing new donors, many arts organizations are hoping to fill the income gap with new sources of earned revenue—food service, parking fees, electronic distribution, and merchandise. In my observation very few arts organizations have enough demand for their products and services to create truly profitable businesses. Frequently these ventures serve the public and the organization's mission, but rarely do they provide much extra revenue for their coffers.

In the face of increasing costs, bounded revenues, and stagnating fund-raising most arts organizations turn eventually to cutting expenses. This makes sense. But the choice of where to cut has huge implications for the organization. It appears easiest to cut those areas that do not require massive reorganization or staff cuts: artistic initiative and marketing. One can mount one less production, mount smaller productions, cut a bit on advertising or public relations expenses, and no one will be the wiser. Wrong.

When one cuts artistic initiative and marketing, one cuts the very reason people supply revenue to the arts organization. Audience members and donors are attracted to exciting, important work; their interest is confirmed by attention generated by marketing efforts. When art and marketing are sacrificed to balance budgets, the organization virtually always suffers a loss in revenue. This results in more cutting, more "saving," more losses, and a vicious spiral is created that has damaged more arts organizations than one can count.

I have spent my career addressing these situations. I have been invited to help numerous organizations that had fallen into the trap of cutting artistic and marketing spending and suffering the consequences. As both chief executive and a consultant I have worked to overcome the challenges imposed by poor spending decisions. I have been associated with so many turnarounds that the press, beginning with Sid Smith in the *Chicago Tribune*, have dubbed me "the Turnaround King."

This book addresses both the theory and the practice of creating a turnaround in the performing arts. The first chapter reviews the major theoretical approaches to changing the fortunes of a performing arts organization. The following chapters present case studies of four of the organizations I have helped to fix: Kansas City Ballet, Alvin Ailey Dance Theater Foundation, American Ballet Theatre, and the Royal Opera House.

The approaches I have developed over the past twenty years are also applicable to "healthy" arts organizations. The sad fact of life is that there is a very slim line between sickness and health in the arts. Organizations that appear robust can suffer dramatic losses quickly and can be thrust into the turnaround position quickly.

So it is imperative that even organizations not facing critical issues behave in ways that prevent future artistic and financial difficulties. For this reason I have included a fifth case study, of the John F. Kennedy Center for the Performing Arts. The management techniques and strategies I have employed in my most recent position are the same ones I have used in more critical situations. And the impact has been as dramatic.

Ultimately, it is not the financial health of an arts organization that is of prime concern. It is the ability of the organization to address its mission. But I have yet to see a performing arts organization that can consistently and vigorously pursue its mission if it is in immediate danger of closing its doors.

While there may never be a shortage of employment for those who fix troubled arts organizations, this is not always happy work. The pain of the troubled arts organization can be intense; angry creditors, disappointed audience members, and disaffected donors create an environment for those within the organization that is compounded by fears of not being paid and the frustration of not pursuing the mission with vigor.

In fact, the reason most arts professionals forgo the higher wages at for-profit ventures is to have some control over the mission of their organizations. When this ability is diminished, job satisfaction plummets.

Therefore, troubled arts organizations are angry, sad, and defeated. It is extremely painful to become involved with them. The entire organization focuses on the size of the problem, the cause of the problem, and whom to blame. Since the manifestation of the problem is frequently centered on how to pay past-due bills, a great deal of effort is spent looking backward. The conversation inside the organization, and too frequently outside as well, is about the problems faced by the company. This very often spills over into the press. Questions about blame, debt, and despair fill the newspapers, doing nothing to encourage anyone to come to the rescue. Well-meaning board members try to take over to solve the problems they believe are caused by an incompetent staff. Staff members complain that if the board gave or raised more money the problems would not exist. The staff is concerned that they will not be paid on time and the board believes that given the crisis the staff should not expect to receive full payment. The staff can't believe that the wealthy board members are so cavalier about their livelihoods. The artistic staff is fighting with the administrators, who are frightened to spend anything and try to dampen the dreams of the artists. The artists are convinced that if only the administrators did a better job of fund-raising and marketing, all would be well. Each department begins to hoard its own supplies and fights for its own small piece of available resources so coordination between departments is virtually impossible. Donors start to pull away, as do board members who become embarrassed about the public problems of the organization. Fixing these organizations is not for the faint of heart.

But in the end, it is all worth it, of course. The power and energy and excitement when a troubled arts organization truly turns the corner and can look to the future rather than dwell on the past create as intensely satisfying a moment as I have experienced. The Alvin Ailey organization recently opened a new facility, a world-class dance building in Midtown Manhattan. Who could have imagined that just fifteen years ago? Even more surprising, just ten years after it almost closed, the Royal Opera House is considered the model of performing arts management in England.

When I began my career, I found turning around arts organizations challenging, rewarding, and something of an ego boost. Today the feelings are far less personal. In 1994 I was fortunate to meet and be a consultant for a remarkable man, Barney Simon, who created the most important theater in South Africa, the Market Theatre. Barney used theater to teach the world about the horrors of apartheid. Barney taught me the difference between producing art and producing change. He believed fervently that those of us who are fortunate enough to be a part of the arts world have an obligation to see past our own successes and to look to the needs of society. He made me understand that turning around arts organizations had less to do with putting another feather in my own cap than with making sure the world was a better place.

It is to Barney's memory I dedicate this book.

THE ART OF THE TURNAROUND

THE ART OF THE TURNAROUND

TEN RULES

All turnarounds are different and yet all turnarounds are the same. While the size of the problem, the organization's visibility, the involvement of government agencies, and the personalities of the key players may vary, in almost every case, one enters an organization that is suffering from poor cash flow, negative press, and angry artists, staff, donors, and board members. The specific strategies that will solve the problem will depend upon the characteristics of the organization, but I have found that there are ten rules that apply to every turnaround. Ignore any one of them at your peril!

I. SOMEONE MUST LEAD

In most troubled arts organizations, the role of leader has become divided into two or more (usually warring) camps. Rather than the "strong volunteer chairperson supporting a dynamic and committed staff head" model that healthy arts organizations enjoy, troubled organizations typically suffer from a diffused leadership structure as numerous parties try to "help." Often board members come to believe that the staff is not competent and begin to poach on the staff's territory. When I arrived at the Royal Opera House, for example, the board met *weekly* for several hours. A portion of this time was devoted to editing press releases and performing other mundane tasks that are truly the work of the staff. But if board members are scared about the future of the organization and doubt the capabilities of the staff, they tend to jump in to fill the breach.

At the same time, the staff is often making decisions without board involvement because "the board has not been as helpful as it should be" and because the board, without the day-to-day knowledge of the staff, typically does not develop reasonable solutions. When several different people feel empowered to make crucial decisions, there can be no real progress as the various parties pursue their own priorities and waste scarce resources.

Someone must be selected to run the turnaround. This person must have a single unified vision for the organization, have the courage to make difficult decisions in the face of controversy, possess strong negotiating skills, respect all parties including artists, work incredibly hard, and have an obsessive focus on solving the problem. This person must also understand marketing, fund-raising, and financial management. It is a hard job description to meet but the job cannot be divided among many people.

I have been asked to play this role numerous times in my career. I have found that entering from the outside made it easier to succeed since I had no history with any organization I have managed; I had no preconceived notions, no embedded allies or enemies, and no motive except to see the organization prosper.

I was fortunate that in every case my board gave me the authority I needed to preside over the turnaround. Had this not been the case, I would not have succeeded. Before a board can cede authority to one individual, especially an outsider, it must truly understand that it needs a turnaround. One would think that this should not be a problem since so many people—staff, board, donors, press—talk about the many failings and cash concerns are so prominent. And yet, I have observed many organizations that are not willing to make the dramatic changes necessary to fix their central problems. It is only when the organization reaches a true crisis point that they recognize a major change is required. This is typically the point at which I am hired.

2. THE LEADER MUST HAVE A PLAN

The leader needs a plan, and fast. The leader cannot simply be strong, determined, and charming. The leader must have a tangible road map that suggests how the organization will become a functioning and stable organism once again. And this plan must be communicated early and often to all the various stakeholders: artists, staff, board, volunteers, press, government agencies, and audience.

The plan must set priorities: it need not focus on every shortcoming of the organization. In almost every turnaround there are three or four key issues that must be addressed. While the result of a period of poor performance typically is that many areas are neglected, not every area is of equal strategic importance. Rarely have I seen a new computer system produce a turnaround, for example.

The plan must include

- An explicit discussion of the mission of the organization. If the goals of the organization are not clearly delineated, and priorities clearly set, it will be impossible to develop a suitable plan.
- A cogent review of the environment in which the organization operates. Without an understanding of the constraints and opportunities presented by the outside world, it is difficult to create a strong game plan.
- An honest evaluation of the strengths and weaknesses of the organization. This must give due credit to the assets of the organization while maturely and forthrightly delineating the weaknesses.
- A coherent set of strategies that will help the organization achieve its mission given the environment in which it operates and its own assets and liabilities.
- A detailed implementation plan that assigns responsibility for every strategy to one or several stakeholders.
- A financial plan that reveals the fiscal implications of the plan.

While plans will differ and be specific to individual organizations, I have found that there are many similarities across organizations. The underlying economic problems of the performing arts suggest that those who provide revenue to arts organizations possess a great deal of power. Audience members have numerous entertainment choices, and the options keep growing every day. And donors have many opportunities to give away their funds since there is no shortage of arts and other not-for-profit organizations competing for these funds. As a result, arts organizations find themselves in the position of supplicant—begging people to buy tickets or donate money.

Any business strategist would tell you that the way to handle strong buyers is to find ways to weaken them. Luckily, in the arts, we have two levers to push to help weaken our buyers: creating unique and exciting programming and marketing this programming very aggressively. Despite the glut of entertainment options, when audience members and donors are excited about a particular performance, that performance will sell tickets and receive funding. This excitement arises from a great idea that is intelligently marketed. For this reason, my mantra for running successful arts organizations is, *Good art, well marketed*. It is really as simple as that. I have yet to see an arts organization that produces excellent art and knows how to market that art aggressively that does not create the financial strength needed to pursue its mission in a consistent manner.

And, ironically, troubled arts organizations must focus on art more than healthy ones. When I arrived at American Ballet Theatre (ABT), we literally had to loosen every second light bulb because we could not afford electricity and we asked all staff to reuse paper by turning it over and using the blank side. And yet, shortly after my arrival, we announced the largest artistic project in our history—a new full-length ballet of *Othello* to a commissioned score. This was one of the most important things we did to turn around ABT. By announcing this project we convinced many people that we had a plan, that we were confident about our future, and that we were a vital, interesting arts organization.

I recently visited a new performing arts organization that is having financial challenges because its artistic product is not strong enough. In an effort to balance the budget for next year, the staff has cut back on the art even further. One does not need to be a turnaround expert to know what is going to happen to this organization.

But this is not a unique case. Just before I arrived at the Royal Opera House my Board had cancelled every performance for the next year and a half! You can imagine the message this delivered to anyone still caring about the institution.

Even healthy organizations must focus on programming. The Kennedy Center was not a sick organization when I arrived in 2001, but the programming was not important enough to generate widespread interest and support. We now spend more than $100 million each year on performing arts programming and education. As a result our contributed income has doubled over six years and we have earned an operating surplus every one of those years.

It helps, of course, if that well-marketed good art is supported by an infrastructure that helps raise money and sell tickets, governs itself, and plans successfully on an ongoing basis. These supporting activities are important foundations for success. But if the art is bad, or if it is not marketed appropriately, then this foundation is not enough to create success.

In the end, the plan must focus on creating a self-sustaining organization. My goal for any organization is to create a *system* that works. This system starts with strong programming, supports it with aggressive marketing, and produces revenue that is invested in better programming that creates more revenue, and on and on. I refer to this cycle as the "engine." Typically in a troubled organization one or more elements of this cycle are broken and must be fixed. This broken element becomes the focus of my plan and the object of my obsessive need to fix the organization.

3. YOU CANNOT SAVE YOUR WAY TO HEALTH

The first inclination of most boards and staffs is that they will save their organizations by saving money. There is a widely held, but usually wrong, belief among board members that artistic leaders are spendthrifts who do not appreciate the difficulty finding funding. Other staff members in the organization are "tarred with the same brush." This condescending line of reasoning results in a belief that if "a businesslike person" attacks the budget, the fat will be removed and the organization will be right-sized.

Nothing could be further from the truth. In only the rarest instance is excessive spending the true root of the problems of an arts organization. In fact, arts organizations have learned to do more with far less than other organizations or corporations. Just evaluate how famous major arts organizations have become with marketing budgets a very small fraction of the size of equally famous corporate entities. And not-for-profit production budgets are virtually always far smaller than those of commercial entertainment endeavors.

This does not mean that savings cannot be achieved in most not-for-profit organizations. When I arrived at the Royal Opera House we had too many layers of management and too many departments that provided luxurious service to the institution. It was essential that these be eliminated. And when I arrived at the Kennedy Center, too much money was spent on conferences, staff trips and meals, and other perquisites that an arts organization cannot afford if it is to produce important programming.

Budget cuts might be advisable but *where* one cuts is crucial. Cutting into non-strategic costs is beneficial; cutting those activities that lead to revenue is foolhardy. But the amounts saved by cutting expenditures on non-strategic areas rarely change the fortunes of a troubled organization. While it is scary for many board members to acknowledge this, cutting these costs does not create my "engine." Revenue is the problem with most arts organizations, not cost. Organizations focused simply on reducing costs will continue to get smaller and smaller and will never create the economic engine that is required for long-term stability and growth.

4. FOCUS ON TODAY AND TOMORROW, NOT YESTERDAY

There are so many things to worry about when one attempts to change the fortunes of a troubled arts organization. First, one must attend to current cash concerns. In fact, addressing short-term cash flow problems can take hours out of every day—talking with vendors, negotiating payout deals, securing funding, estimating cash flows, and so on. I once had a ballet shoe vendor sit at my desk at American Ballet Theatre and refuse to leave until I had written him a check. It is the irony of the turnaround that one wastes so much time on cash flow issues exactly at the point one needs time to implement the programs that will create health.

It would be naïve to suggest that this time is not required, however. It is the cost to the troubled organization for making financial commitments it could not fulfill. The fear and pain of not making payroll, not meeting vendor payment plans, and not having the resources needed to continue to function have sent me to the bottle (of hair dye, that is). And a thoughtful, open, and fair approach to unpaid vendors can lead to payment plans that are affordable. In fact, I have found that a strategic plan is the best tool available to convince vendors that the organization has an approach to finding the resources required to pay them.

But the true turnaround artist possesses the discipline to carve out time each week to focus on artistic programming, board development, donor and press cultivation, and other activities that will make future years easier. Too many executives spend *all* of their time on short-term issues. If making this week's payroll is one's sole focus, next week is certain to be more difficult. The institutional marketing program we installed at Alvin Ailey, the new production of *Othello* we created at ABT, and the re-opening programs we developed for the Royal Opera House were central to revitalizing these organizations, but it took great discipline to invest time in these activities when the short-term outlook was so bleak.

What one must *not* do is waste time rehashing the past, pointing fingers, and looking for scapegoats. These activities stall all progress and deflate the hope and optimism that can emerge from the planning process. Historians do not make turnaround kings!

5. EXTEND YOUR PROGRAMMING PLANNING CALENDAR

Too many arts organizations plan their programming only one or two years in advance, and troubled organizations typically *reduce* this time frame. Many arts executives have suggested it would be foolhardy to plan further into the future since the future seems so uncertain. This has been an argument I have heard most often among smaller institutions both in the United States and around the world.

And yet, if one does not plan far into the future, it is virtually impossible to develop the large, exciting projects that will reinvigorate the audience and donors. When one creates programming ideas years into the future:

1. You can ensure that the artists you want to work with are available.
2. You are far more likely to raise the funding required for a large project.
3. You are far more likely to get important advance press.
4. You are far more likely to negotiate a successful tour.

Long-term artistic planning also gives artistic leaders and administrators a chance to discuss programming without the pressure of short-term financial considerations. It helps foster the bond that is required between these two sets of individuals.

I keep a very simple piece of paper within easy reach at all times. It lists the important projects under consideration for the next five years. I review this page over and over, constantly worrying about ways to strengthen the programming. And I share some of this information with selected donors and prospects. Nothing helps raising money more than presenting a menu of programming ideas that gives important donors a choice. Too many arts administrators go to a prospect with one project to "sell." I never go to a prospect meeting with fewer than ten projects in mind.

In developing these programming ideas, I focus on projects that seem exciting and worthy of press attention and funding. I also work to reduce the risk associated with any possible project. Risky programming is great; risky operations are not. One way to reduce operational risk is to create joint ventures with other organizations. Well-designed joint ventures allow both organizations to benefit from the strengths of the other entity. The ABT production of *Othello* was a joint venture with the San Francisco Ballet. This reduced our costs by half and ensured a life for the ballet beyond our initial performances.

6. MARKETING IS MORE THAN BROCHURES AND ADVERTISEMENTS

If there is one thing I have done to help the troubled organizations I have managed it has been to create a very aggressive and systematic marketing program. While it is crucial for arts organizations to develop important new artistic and educational programs, it is also vital that these programs be marketed in sophisticated and creative ways.

Too many arts organizations pay marketing attention to projects only when there is earned revenue at stake. This *programmatic* marketing is central to building earned income—the brochures, advertisements, posters, emails, and so forth, that sell tickets must be designed and distributed intelligently and with a goal of reaching the potential buyer.

But too few organizations spend any time or effort performing *institutional* marketing, the marketing of the entire institutional image that gets people excited about supporting the company. While institutional marketing can help sell tickets (people visit La Scala in Milan because it *is* La Scala; this reduces the amount the organization must spend on programmatic marketing), it has a bigger role in increasing contributed income. There are many ways to increase institutional visibility: special gala performances, unusual exhibitions and lectures, the use of celebrities, important performance and education programming that captures the imagination of the press, appearances on important television and radio programs, stories in major print outlets, and involvement in high-visibility public functions.

While many of these techniques represent an intersection with programmatic marketing, most organizations do not create a systematic program of public relations and other activities aimed at increasing institutional visibility. I believe large organizations should have at least one "hit" a month, not a small mention in a newspaper but a major event or press coverage that impresses donors and prospects about the importance of the organization. Smaller organizations should aim for one hit each quarter.

Not every event must be featured in the press to have an impact. I believe that there are a few hundred people in a community who can affect the future of any arts organization. While one influences large numbers of people when the press covers your events, you can create great awareness among very potent people with private events as well.

This must not be left to chance. Although the decision of any one journalist to feature your organization is not within your control, creating an institutional marketing plan that includes performances and events that are likely to interest the press and your donor base is achievable by any organization. I meet every morning with my heads of press and marketing to discuss how we are going to create this coverage every month into the future. I do not leave this to chance. If there is a substantial hole in a given month, we develop a plan for filling it.

As a result, my organizations become more exciting, more vital, and sexier to their home communities; this results in far more financial support as well. We created a major, year-long program for Alvin Ailey that allowed New Yorkers to appreciate us far more than in the past. This included appearances on television, major free events, museum exhibitions, and all-star galas. As a result, our fund-raising doubled.

The Kansas City Ballet arranged a tour to New York City, invited three national dance magazines to write stories, formed a relationship with a noontime television news show, and appeared several times a year on an early morning interview show. The deficit of the company was paid off in one season.

The Royal Opera House, which had the worst reputation of any arts organization imaginable, was about to open a newly renovated opera house. We turned the discussion from past problems to future opportunities by promoting the opera house to come and the largest arts education program in the nation. The entire thirty-million-dollar deficit was erased in two years.

These institutional marketing efforts played a central role in the turnaround efforts of these organizations. They must play a part in every turnaround.

7. THERE MUST BE ONLY ONE SPOKESMAN AND THE MESSAGE MUST BE POSITIVE

If institutional marketing is central to a turnaround, then controlling the message by controlling the messenger is also crucial. One of the challenges faced by troubled arts organizations is that the public begins to hear from a variety of disgruntled voices. It is not unusual for artists, board members, staff members, and others to talk with the press about the problems facing the organization. The Royal Opera House was the most famous, although not the only, instance of this. An entire cadre of newspaper reporters made a career of writing of the woes of the Opera House. Many of them camped out in pubs across the street to make sure they heard the latest gossip from staff members, board members, and artists. When Lincoln Center went through some difficult times in the early years of this century, many constituents were heard from as well.

When so many people are communicating with the press, no one is controlling the message. News reports, therefore, become focused solely on the problems, when they occurred, and who caused them. This focus only exacerbates the problem. Those donors or audience members still loyal to the organization become embarrassed and are dissuaded from continuing their support, and attracting new donors becomes virtually impossible.

Negative news coverage discourages your supporters from involving their friends and associates even if they continue their own personal support. When I arrived at Alvin Ailey (or ABT or the Royal Opera House) I found that not one member of my board knew anyone to solicit. When our problems had evaporated two years later, all of a sudden everyone knew lots of people to approach. When your supporters become "unembarrassed" they become so much more potent.

The message for every arts organization must focus on its reason for being, its mission. And the news that is broadcast must focus on the wonderful projects that the organization is planning to support this mission, rather than on the latest financial crisis. This is one reason why planning programming far in advance is such an important turnaround technique.

At American Ballet Theatre we used a special challenge grant from our chairman to change the nature of our public image.

At the Kansas City Ballet, where an entire community thought of us as unable to manage ourselves, we changed our message by presenting our new strategic plan at a special cocktail party for donors and civic leaders.

Every arts organization has good news to share; most are not aggressive enough about making sure their positive messages are heard. I was called "Pollyanna," "Mary Poppins," and all sorts of similar names in the British press. Before I arrived at the Royal Opera House, they were being fed a steady diet of bad news. After I was hired, I only talked about the wonderful new opera house we were building.

In every turnaround situation I enter, I have one rule: I am the only one who decides who speaks to the press. When the British press had no access to anyone but positive Pollyanna Michael, the nature of our coverage changed: from "Chaos Reigns as Kaiser Enters Opera House" to "Miracle at the Garden."

8. FUND-RAISING MUST FOCUS ON THE LARGER DONOR, BUT DON'T AIM TOO HIGH

In my experience, turnarounds rely far more heavily on increasing fund-raising revenue than they do on increasing ticket sales. This does not mean it is not helpful to take in more money at the box office or to enjoy a more profitable tour schedule. But I have found that few organizations in need of turnarounds can earn enough extra to pay off debts and establish fiscal health.

But turnarounds must take place with energy and speed. It is difficult for any organization to maintain the necessary focus and energy that a turnaround demands for more than three years. The focus of the fund-raising efforts, therefore, must be on gifts that are large enough to make a difference. While small contributions are always appreciated, they are not sufficient to make a dent in the deficit.

On the other hand, aiming to fill a deficit with one extraordinary gift is usually just a pipe dream. When I got to Alvin Ailey, my board told me that I should ask Bill Cosby to write a check for $1 million and that would solve our problems. Actually $1 million was not enough to cover our needs. But more important, Mr. Cosby had no reason to give such a large gift to an organization that could not raise more than $1,000 from most of its board members. He also would not give and should not have given a big gift to an organization that was a mess.

In other words, we need to focus on "right-sized gifts," gifts that make sense given the budget and the profile of the organization. For Ailey with a $6 million budget and a $1.5 million deficit, $50 was too low and $1 million was too high. At Ailey, while we did receive larger gifts, we focused our fund-raising on $1,000 gifts. Our board felt comfortable asking this amount from friends and associates, and this was an amount that would make a difference to us. (Of course when developing any fund-raising plan, but certainly during a turnaround, one must make sure the cost of fulfilling all promises to the donors falls well short of the gift size; this is another reason to focus on larger gifts.) Within six weeks we had doubled the level of individual giving to the organization and had paid off a substantial portion of our deficit.

At the Kennedy Center, with an unearned income target of $70 million each year, I must focus on far larger gifts. Our major growth has resulted from gifts that exceed $50,000 a year; this has allowed us to double our fund-raising over the past six years.

I ask those donors willing and able to make a truly substantial gift to structure it as a challenge grant, obligating the organization to match all or a part of the gift with other contributions. We employed this technique to great effect at ABT. One challenge grant from our chairman raised virtually all the money needed to pay off a very substantial deficit.

I have been very vocal in suggesting matching grants to every funder and government agency that will listen. I believe this is especially important in other countries that are trying to encourage private fund-raising to supplement government funding.

9. THE BOARD MUST ALLOW ITSELF
TO BE RESTRUCTURED

If the fund-raising activity is key to the turnaround, then the board's potency must be an issue as well. Boards provide a vital underpinning to the fund-raising success of most arts organizations, especially with individual and corporate donors. Frequently, an arts organization gets sick because it has not enjoyed the evolution of the board's fund-raising power that is required as the organization and its budget grow.

When an organization is young, the board will typically be composed of friends and family of the artistic visionary who starts the organization. These friends typically act as quasi-staff and perform tasks that staff members will perform as the organization matures. As this maturation progresses, board membership must migrate toward people who can find new resources and can provide support of their own.

A board of a turnaround candidate must evaluate in a clear, mature, and honest fashion whether its membership can provide and raise the resources needed by the organization at that point in its history.

When I arrived at the Alvin Ailey organization, half of our thirty-six board members gave less than $500 a year to this important dance company, which had a budget exceeding $6 million a year. This simply was not satisfactory. When we imposed a giving requirement of $10,000 we lost half of our board members, but we were able to replace them with people who could support the organization in the way that was required. These new board members also introduced new contacts and new energy to the organization. They were not weighed down by pessimism and exhaustion.

In fact, when I applied for the job I was told by several board members that my idea that the organization should be able to raise more than $1.7 million a year was unrealistic. I believed that the most important modern dance organization in the world and the largest African-American cultural institution should have claim on more contributed income. In fact, two years later we doubled that amount and since the early 1990s, this amount has doubled several times over.

The heart of this growth was the restructuring of the board. We got rid of the dead weight, hired new members, gave a clear orientation, were explicit about our needs, created a workable plan, helped our board members raise funds, and did the marketing and programming that made them excited to participate. The new board members also spurred the more senior members to greater involvement.

This all required substantial staff time, but this was time well spent. I believe that a senior staff person should communicate with every productive board member at least six times a year. If this is not happening, it means that either the board is too large or the staff does not appreciate their role in creating a strong and involved board.

10. THE ORGANIZATION MUST HAVE THE DISCIPLINE TO FOLLOW EACH OF THESE RULES

There is not one of these rules that can be sacrificed in the pursuit of a turnaround. All are equally important. This puts the leaders of turnarounds in a difficult situation. They must be able to balance many competing needs at the same time. They must deal with the current, short-term cash needs while also addressing the future. They must deal with the great stress induced by these problems while also presenting a strong and upbeat face to the outside world. They must present solutions rather than problems to anyone who has the power to help: board members, staff members, donors, and the public. They must also work quickly and rather ruthlessly to make the changes necessary. Truly troubled arts organizations do not have the time for consensus building, numerous staff meetings, or focus groups. They require quick, smart, determined action. Not everyone in the organization will agree with the leader or even like the leader. But, ideally, at the end of the turnaround, all will respect that something miraculous has transpired.

In fact, turnarounds are not miracles. They result from good planning and determined implementation. And from a severe lack of sleep.

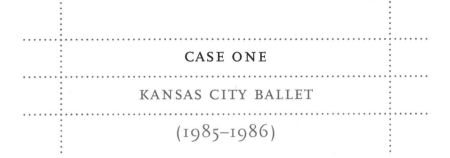

CASE ONE

KANSAS CITY BALLET

(1985–1986)

In the summer of 1985 I sold Michael M. Kaiser Associates, a management consulting firm I opened in 1981. The firm offered strategic planning support to numerous Fortune 500 corporations. We specialized in studying the way industries were evolving and the strategies competitors were embracing to respond.

While the work was interesting and the business was highly profitable, I was traveling six days a week and enjoying the client interaction less and less. One day I found myself lying on the floor of the Detroit airport looking up at a group of concerned faces; I had collapsed. It was time to make some changes.

The first thing I did was to seek out some other outlet for my energy and time. I called the Washington Opera, a growing opera company housed at the Kennedy Center, and asked for a meeting with its general director, Martin Feinstein. I told Martin that I was happy to contribute to the opera but that I wanted to play some sort of volunteer role as well. I had expertise in planning and was happy to contribute my planning expertise as well as my money. The timing was fortuitous. The opera was applying for a Challenge Grant from the National Endowment for the Arts and a strategic plan was a required element of the application. He asked whether I would help them write the plan. It was the most exciting project I could have imagined.

I knew absolutely nothing about running an opera company, but I did know how to ask questions and to assemble data and plans. With the great help of the staff, we developed a thorough plan to suggest the way this rapidly growing opera company could create new resources and new audiences. I was asked to join the board and eventually the executive committee. I cannot overstate how much I learned through this activity.

But as a young, immature, conceited management consultant I did not appreciate the proper place of a board member. I became involved in issues that were truly staff concerns, stirred up other board members, and made a general nuisance of myself. Martin put up with me because I was being generous, but I was clearly a pest.

Over time it became clear to me that the role of board member was not sufficient to meet my artistic needs and ambitions. And I was growing less and less interested in the work of Kaiser Associates. I asked my business partner to consider buying me out. He was doing very well financially at the firm and had developed into a seriously good consultant. He decided to take the plunge and buy me out and I was out of the firm within two months.

However, while my "portfolio" of skills was broad, it was not deep. I knew a good amount about financial modeling and strategic planning and a bit about managing people. I was a good presenter and not a bad salesman, and I had served on the board of one arts organization for just over one year: hardly the profile to excite search committees of major arts organizations. While I was realistic about my lack of arts management experience, I felt I had progressed far enough in my career to obtain a responsible position and was not prepared to accept work as a secretary or junior-level manager.

The arts world is not an easy one to enter, however. Jobs are relatively scarce, and, while they turn over rapidly, the market for job applicants is not very efficient; there are simply not enough jobs to justify the array of recruiting services that exist for larger industries. And while the Internet has provided new avenues for advertising job openings, small arts organizations typically do not cast their nets very wide when they are looking for new administrators. Both the organization and the job seeker have to network. Apart from a few people at the Washington Opera, however, my network was remarkably small. Ironically, it was one of my Kaiser Associates clients who helped me enter the arts management field.

In my last few weeks at Kaiser Associates I informed each client of my plans. Most of my clients thought I was absolutely insane. Why would I leave the safe, profitable world of consulting to enter the inefficient, unimportant world of the arts? In their minds, and in the minds of many corporate executives, managing an arts organization, even a large one, was one step up from running the PTA bake sale.

One of my best clients was United Telecommunications in Kansas City, Missouri. I worked with several executives there, including a young executive named Bob Richards. Bob sat on the board of the Kansas City Ballet, a mid-sized regional ballet company that had been through four managers in as many years of existence as a professional company. The company was on the verge of bankruptcy. Would I be interested?

With no other prospects in sight, yet with absolutely no knowledge of ballet, I said yes. At my own expense (the board leadership thought I was such an outlandish candidate that they could not justify paying for my travel) I flew to Kansas City at the end of July 1985. That trip seemed very strange at the time but I have come to realize that most searches in the arts are a bit unusual. Why? Because the board members entrusted with hiring the senior artistic and executive managers are frequently arts amateurs. While they may be wonderful supporters of the arts, and of the arts institution, they often have little idea about the true workings of the institution or what it takes to be a strong arts manager. They can feel when the organization is functioning smoothly but they don't truly understand the required job skills. The search committees of many boards, unless they have professional executive recruitment support (and most cannot afford it), usually are flying blind. And the individual prejudices of the committee members, and especially of the chair, tend to sway the decisions. All too frequently, board members who are concerned for the fiscal health of an organization seek an individual with a finance rather than arts management background. Almost as frequently, these appointments fail.

Hiring and firing top managers are two of the key roles of the board members of a not-for-profit arts organization, and yet no one bothers to teach them how to do it and what to look for. It is not a surprise, therefore, that many new top arts executives are ousted before their second year in service.

The Kansas City Ballet search committee was no exception. They were a kind, supportive, interested group of amateurs, all with their own agendas. The company had a strong artistic team but a largely unsophisticated management team and was in danger of extinction. It had debts of more than $125,000 and the staff regularly had to phone around to find the cash to cover the dancers' weekly payroll. The twenty-six dancers were only earning an average of $350 a week so this payroll was not particularly onerous. But if you don't have any cash, and owe a good deal, any amount seems large. The company had been phoning its major supporters so often for emergency contributions that goodwill had eroded and the company had become something of a local joke. It was terribly unfair to the artists, but bad management always affects the artists more than it does the executives, who typically have more employment options.

As with most troubled organizations, the board believed that the problem lay with the artistic management. They thought the company needed to "do more popular repertoire," spend less money, and get more efficient. I listened to their comments and only replied that if I were hired, the first thing we would do would be to create a plan that would detail our way forward. I was not at all experienced in dance and I had no idea why this organization was in trouble, but I certainly was not impressed with the "insights" I was hearing.

In the course of my two-day visit, I heard more about the failings of the fellow board members than about the organization. I was hardly "interviewed" at all. The chair of the search committee asked after scanning my resume, "Can't you hold a job?" It was a fair question, for I had left a variety of positions in my young career. (She should only see my resume today!) But the interview, held in her Jaguar as she drove me to my hotel, went no further. A local bank executive was a good friend of Bob Richards and was "pre-sold." The treasurer of the board was an accountant who appreciated my finance background. His primary interest was in how he could become a better fund-raiser. The chairman of the board could not understand why I would want the position at all. He could not wait to complete his term as chairman.

The toughest questioning was that by the artistic director, Todd Bolender. Todd, of course, had the most to gain or lose from this appointment. He had moved to Kansas City in 1981. A former George Balanchine dancer and protégé, Todd was an important person in the ballet world. Balanchine had created major roles for him (including Phlegmatic in *The Four Temperaments*), and Todd had choreographed works for the New York City Ballet. Before going to Kansas City, he had worked extensively in Europe. Todd expected a very high standard of quality and was able to draw a number of his notable friends to Kansas City to work with the company. In my time there, Millicent Hayden, Janet Reed, John Taras, and Violette Verdy all came to Kansas City. In many respects, the Kansas City community did not understand what a treasure they had in Todd and certainly were not supporting the company well enough to justify his huge commitment.

Todd had assembled a strong artistic team in Una Kai, former ballet mistress for both Balanchine and Robert Joffrey, and Diana Adams, who ran the Kansas City Ballet School. Diana had been one of the important New York City Ballet dancers of the 1950s and 1960s, known for her beautiful legs and strong technique. The three of them sat in Todd's office and grilled me. They were skeptical that this "businessman" would be sensitive to their needs. They thought I would simply be a tool of the board, telling them that they could not spend any money on dancers, new productions, or the school. I spent hours trying to convince them of my passion for the arts, my desire to support their artistic goals, and my independence from the board.

It must have worked. Within a week I was offered the job and I immediately accepted even though my annual salary was less than my *weekly* income at Kaiser Associates. (My poor accountant still has not recovered from that shock.) By the last week of August 1985, less than two months after I had decided to leave the consulting world behind, I left my home in Washington and moved with my two dogs to Kansas City. I was now an arts manager.

The Kansas City Ballet was housed at the Westport Allen Center, an old public school that had been converted into a home for a variety of charities, including a drug rehabilitation support group. With three studios, offices and dressing rooms, twenty-six dancers, staff, faculty, and scores of students, the ballet dominated the center physically and spiritually. While Todd and I had our own offices, the remainder of the staff of four—a finance manager, a marketing manager, a box office manager, and a secretary—shared one large room. This small, happy band was the administration of the Kansas City Ballet. We had a part-time fund-raiser who quit soon after my arrival and left no fund-raising records whatsoever.

We also had no real marketing strategy, no profile in the community, and no money. We had a small subscription base, but all the money for subscriptions for the season about to start had been spent the previous spring to pay off old bills. The company did three programs of shorter works (repertory programs) each year—one in October, one in February, and one in May—and a run of *Nutcrackers* in December. Like most other ballet companies in the United States, without *Nutcracker*, we would have been insolvent.

Unfortunately the company had not paid the rent on the theater for *Nutcracker* the year before and we were unceremoniously informed my first month on the job that if we did not pay last year's rent, there would be no *Nutcracker* this year, and, hence, no Kansas City Ballet.

Welcome to the arts, Michael Kaiser!

Practical person that I am, I realized that the first thing we needed to do was to get some money. And it also seemed evident that we were not going to be able to get any money as long as people believed we were going bankrupt. (This precept of a turnaround is not understood by enough arts executives; threatening bankruptcy is not the way to create fiscal health.) We needed to attack this problem in two ways: we had to convince the major individual donors and the business community that we understood our problems and were acting in a professional way to address them, and we had to convince the audience that we were an exciting and important part of the local cultural scene. In the short term, we were much more successful achieving the first goal than the second.

Kansas City is a relatively small town. At the time I arrived, it was the smallest city in the United States to have both major league baseball and football franchises. In fact, the Kansas City Royals won the World Series shortly after I arrived, but more of that later. It appeared that changing the minds of the community leaders about the Kansas City Ballet would require communicating with only a few hundred individuals. (I have since learned this is true for just about every arts organization.) This seemed doable. I believed that we needed to convince these few people that the company was of a high artistic quality, that we had a path to fiscal stability, and that the community should be proud enough of this company to support it as we worked to achieve this stability.

Convincing people of the artistic quality of the company was a challenge. There was the prevailing feeling in Kansas City, as in many cities, that the only really good art was created on the coasts (and, perhaps, Chicago) and that despite the pedigrees of the artistic leaders, anything local was, by definition, simply of civic quality. But the local museum, the Nelson-Atkins Museum, had successfully convinced everyone of its quality, so I knew it could be done. Luckily all three major national dance publications (*Dance Magazine*, *Ballet Review*, and, now defunct, *Ballet News*) were in the process of writing feature stories about the Kansas City Ballet. I simply had to let people know about this, and I did so, endlessly. Reprints of every important article were sent to those few hundred people I believed could change our history. I also negotiated a tour to New York City, making the Kansas City Ballet the first arts organization from that town to perform in the nation's arts capital. This was big news.

Showing that we had a path to fiscal stability was easier. In record time (less than two months) I wrote a strategic plan for the organization and had it reviewed and approved by a board planning committee and the full board. The plan suggested that we make the Kansas City Ballet the city's chief cultural export. The New York tour was one element; building a long-term residence in St. Louis was another. A program for expanded marketing and more active fund-raising was also included. The plan was "unveiled" to a group of influential business people and community leaders at a cocktail party at the home of one of our board members. We chose his home because it was so beautiful and lavishly decorated and we knew that most people in the community would want to see it. I made a brief speech about the future of the ballet and every attendee received a copy of the plan upon leaving. It was very well received.

The Kansas City Ballet was producing high-quality programming, but it was not marketing itself well. We needed to find ways to get people excited about the Fall Program and about the institution as a whole. I learned about this difference between programmatic marketing (selling the Fall Program) and institutional marketing (selling the entire institution) in a dramatic and painful way.

One board member appreciated the need to improve our marketing and offered to sponsor the cost of engaging a marketing consultant who had had great success marketing a local professional soccer franchise and an annual civic festival. We wanted to find a way to create an image of the company as a hidden local resource. The consultant came up with a campaign that would feature a teaser, "What are the most valuable 52 feet in Kansas City?" This line would be included in advertisements, balloons, and so on, with no attribution. A large banner was to be placed on an overpass leading to downtown. We believed that everyone would assume the "52 feet" referred to a parcel of land and hoped the question would be so provocative that radio stations and newspapers would mention the campaign. After a month or so of building tension, we would answer our own question: the most valuable 52 feet in Kansas City were those belonging to the dancers of the Kansas City Ballet. I appreciated the cleverness of the idea and wanted to believe that it would lead to the coverage the consultant anticipated. (I had, please remember, no experience running an arts organization and had lived in Kansas City for three weeks at the time this campaign was created.) My staff members, especially my finance director, Claudette Donlon, were deeply skeptical.

In the event, it poured the day we launched the campaign, the banner on the overpass fell off after two soggy hours, and no one seemed to notice or care about the small advertisements we could afford to place. What was worse, we used up most of our marketing budget for the Fall Program on the campaign. We had only enough money for a few ads for these performances. The program would be a "hard sell" in any event. It had only one work new to the company, a staging of Todd's *Miraculous Mandarin*, a very dark and difficult ballet. All of the other works were already familiar to the audience. Todd wanted to use as the central publicity shot a picture of himself as the Mandarin taken when he created the work for the New York City Ballet. It was meaningful only to a few dance cognoscenti and made no impact on the casual dance goer, another lesson learned. As mentioned earlier, the Kansas City Royals made it to the World Series in 1985 and eventually won a thrilling seven-game series against cross-state rivals the St. Louis Cardinals on my birthday, October 27. The entire city was riveted. Unfortunately, our Fall Program was scheduled to begin four days after the final game, on Halloween, no less.

Whether it was the World Series, Halloween, the difficult program, the lack of marketing, or the choice of photos, the fall season had the worst attendance in Kansas City Ballet history. My debut as an arts manager was not exactly a smash hit. The actual performances went well and the reviews were fine. I was a nervous wreck on opening night, frightened that the curtain would not go up if there were something the executive was supposed to do that I was too inexperienced to have done. I also feared that at the climactic moment in the *Miraculous Mandarin*, when the Mandarin is hanged, the noose would break and our star dancer would be strangled to death. I need not have worried; the staff members and crew were thoroughly professional and had ensured that everything that needed to be done was done and done well.

But there were lessons to be learned. While our consultant was correct in his belief that we had to raise the institutional profile of the company, we could not afford to spend much money to do so. While Todd certainly had to create the programs that he felt met his artistic goals, I needed to have some input about the marketing profile for each program. The selection of images used to market a season had to appeal to our marginal ticket buyers (those who may or may not choose to attend), not to the die-hard fan who would attend anyway. And we needed to find a way to fill large numbers of empty seats in the theater. No marketing program we could afford would, in the short term, increase the percentage of seats sold at full price to an acceptable number.

I decided to mount a full-scale effort to build the community's appreciation for Todd and his dancers. I went on local radio and television constantly. Most local stations were looking for content, and there I was, happily talking about Todd and Una and Diana and the three national publications and the tour to New York. I was a regular guest on a very early morning television interview show that was watched by a large segment of the business community. For this audience, I stressed the improving fiscal health of the organization. On daytime television and radio I focused on the impending production of *Sleeping Beauty* Act 3 that was certain to be a highlight of the Winter Program, and of the forthcoming collaboration with Alvin Ailey. Alvin was giving his ballet *The River* to the Kansas City Ballet for the Spring Program. He was going to coach it himself. This certainly suggested that the company had achieved a certain artistic stature.

It must be obvious that the Kansas City Ballet was a classroom for me. I had no real idea what I was doing and worked from intuition. As helpful as my staff members were, none of them had ever run an arts organization either, and we simply did the best we could. There were signs that we were winning. Fund-raising revenue was increasing, the sense in the community was that we were doing interesting things, and the board was relaxing. Luckily, the *Nutcracker* season went well and the weather cooperated. Except for a few buttons that were misprinted *Nutracker* instead of *Nutcracker* things went without a hitch and the infusion of ticket money eased cash flow concerns for a few weeks.

We were approached by the major dance presenter in St. Louis, Dance St. Louis, about the possibility of establishing a permanent relationship that would take the Kansas City Ballet to St. Louis on a regular basis. As a presenter, Dance St. Louis drew dance companies from around the nation and the world to St. Louis. It did not have a dance company of its own; it raised money so that high-quality dance could be enjoyed in St. Louis. It also mounted educational programs in the area's public schools. Dance St. Louis, like all dance presenters and all touring dance companies, had been adversely affected by the elimination of the National Endowment for the Arts (NEA) dance touring program. The NEA, in a cost-cutting move, eliminated subsidies it had previously given to support the touring of dance companies. This had a devastating impact on the entire dance economy. It was to initiate the problems suffered by the Joffrey Ballet, ABT, and all other touring ballet companies.

The advantages for the Kansas City Ballet of establishing a permanent residence in St. Louis, of course, were more performing opportunities, greater claim on state funds, prestige that would lead to additional touring, and the opportunity to fund-raise in St. Louis. In virtually all American dance companies, dancers are only paid for the weeks they work, plus some vacation payment in larger companies. In many companies, dancers are paid less for weeks of rehearsal than for performance weeks. If you don't dance, you don't get paid. Unionized companies typically have a guaranteed number of weeks of work per year, with something between thirty-six and forty being standard, although there are exceptions. For those companies with guaranteed weeks of work, a central challenge is to fill an appropriate proportion with performance dates since there is no income generated during rehearsal weeks.

For the non-unionized Kansas City dancers, there were no guaranteed weeks of work. While the artistic leadership required a certain amount of time to rehearse, if we did not have performing opportunities (for which a fee was paid by a presenter if on tour, or for which we received ticket revenue if performing at home), we could not employ the dancers. We wanted to find more weeks of work so that we could give our dancers a decent wage, attract better dancers to the company (dancers are not typically going to move to Kansas City if they are only paid a small salary for a few weeks each year), improve the quality of performance, and build the image of the company.

The Kansas City Ballet did not have an active touring program; every year we would have a few dates in smaller cities in Missouri, Kansas, Arkansas, and Nebraska. While we had performed with Dance St. Louis in the past, the possibility of several *guaranteed* visits each year to St. Louis was extremely attractive.

Negotiating the deal was another matter. Dance St. Louis had its own financial challenges and certainly was not in position to pay us huge fees or to allow us to steal its donors. We decided on a reasonable fee for two visits each year, a run of *Nutcracker*s and one repertory program in the spring. We also agreed to mount a summer dance school in St. Louis.

While we did not have great difficulty establishing a fee, the board of Dance St. Louis had one requirement that created a problem: they insisted the company change its name to reflect its new statewide role. The Kansas City Ballet board members were not pleased, but they appreciated the potential of this relationship. The question was, What name? Obviously *Missouri* should be in there somewhere. But the surrounding words created a bitter controversy that raged for weeks and weeks and polarized the board and staff in Kansas City.

Todd, with a background in European dance, wanted the word *State* in the name. I think he hoped that the Missouri government would offer the same support that European governments provide to their state companies. That seemed unlikely to the rest of us.

One board member wanted to name the company the *Royal Ballet of Missouri*. She was not taken seriously. Another insisted the name should be *Ballet Missouri*. She felt this was simple, accurate, and somewhat "trendy." The most popular choice, however, was *Missouri Ballet*. It was simple if not euphonious. Forces lined up on all sides of this issue. (I only realize in hindsight how much progress we had made in a few months' time; rather than arguing about how we should slash the budget, we were arguing over a name!)

And then Todd issued an edict. If the new name were not *State Ballet of Missouri* he would resign. That settled the issue. Todd had been responsible for taking a semiprofessional company and building a strong attractive group of dancers. He had built an artistic team that any dance company would admire and envy. He simply could not leave.

After a great deal of anger, recriminations, and frustration, the Board acquiesced. And that was how the Kansas City Ballet got the awkward name, *State Ballet of Missouri*, or *S-BOM* to the dancers. In truth, no one liked the name. No one could remember it. Most people took to calling it the State of Missouri Ballet. But there it was. (Only years later did the company change its name back to Kansas City Ballet after the relationship with Dance St. Louis was allowed to wither and die.)

While this discussion was under way, we mounted our Winter Program. This included George Balanchine's *Serenade*; Jerome Robbins's *Afternoon of a Faun*; a whimsical ballet by Todd, *Creation of the World*; and *Sleeping Beauty* Act 3. It was a very long and diverse program.

For marketing purposes we focused on *Sleeping Beauty*. (I decided to market this segment as *Sleeping Beauty* Act III rather than the more standard *Aurora's Wedding* because I was convinced that more people would recognize the work by this name.) We knew that there would be demand for this classic. But we also knew we had never sold more than 60 percent of our seats for any repertory program and that was simply not enough. I decided that we needed to find a large group to fill seats, and through discussion and negotiation we found the group that should be the best friend of every ballet company: the Girl Scouts of America. We drew thousands of young girls at reduced prices to the Winter Program. In fact, we sold more than 90 percent of our seats, and the final performance, a Sunday matinee, was completely sold out.

I will always remember with some pride one donor running toward me in the lobby of the Lyric Theater and asking, loudly, why she could not buy a ticket to the performance. After I explained that conditions were changing at the ballet and that in the future people would have to buy in advance, she stormed out, hurling invectives. But I know she was secretly as pleased as I was. My euphoria was a bit tempered by Todd's reaction to the filled houses. "Too much noise," he sniffed.

Kansas City was different from the cities in which I had lived in that there was a very clear social pyramid; your rank was measured by the size of your bank account and home, the country club to which you belonged, and the influence you had in the community. Three families seemed to sit atop the pyramid. Virtually all of them supported the ballet as well as the other major cultural organizations in town: the Kansas City Symphony, the Missouri Repertory Theater, the Kansas City Lyric Opera, and, of course, the Nelson-Atkins Museum. With the same relatively small group of wealthy patrons and corporate executives supporting all of the arts organizations, the competition to be the best, sexiest, and most successful was intense.

This competition was experienced in all aspects of revenue generation and, certainly, in the annual fund-raising event. Each of the organizations had a fund-raiser and the same group of patrons attended each event. There were only a few hotel ballrooms large enough to house these events at that time, and so every event was held in the same spaces with the same catering. How to differentiate? Several years before, our Gala Committee leaders had found a way. They had arranged for all the visual merchandisers of the city's major department stores to work together to design the decor of the Ballet Ball. Each year, in rotation, a different store's visual merchandiser (when I arrived in Kansas City I only knew of them as window dressers) was the chair of the committee and took a leadership role.

In 1986, the designers had outdone themselves; the ballroom of the Alameda Plaza Hotel (now the Fairmont) had several huge pianos flying from the ceiling. It was astonishing. The ballet company did a small performance on a smaller stage, everyone danced and ate and, mostly, drank, and a record amount was raised for the ballet company.

The Ballet Ball, the increase in ticket sales, the sharp increase in fund-raising resulting from the focus on positive publicity in the local media, the forthcoming tour to New York, and the national press attention all were having an impact. The ballet company was certainly the "hot" organization in town, and there was even sentiment that the Kansas City Ballet could be more than a strong local company, that it could have a regional or even a national role. The result was increased support from corporate and private donors alike. The major donors were all happy with our progress and ready to support us. More important, they were encouraging their friends and associates to support us as well.

By March 1986 it seemed that with a strong finish to the season, we actually enjoyed the definite possibility of paying off the entire accumulated deficit of the Kansas City Ballet. The elation that the donors, the dancers, and the entire Kansas City Ballet family began to feel cannot be overstated. The energy released when a chronically troubled arts organization begins to establish financial stability is enormous and potent. Success begets success in most ventures and certainly in those that rely upon charitable contributions.

And the best was still yet to come that season. The season concluded with two noteworthy programs. Our Spring Program featured a lovely new ballet by Todd set to piano music by Chopin and Alvin Ailey's *The River*. *The River* had been created for American Ballet Theatre (to a commissioned score by Duke Ellington) some fifteen years before, originally featuring the great ABT dancers of that time, including Cynthia Gregory. Alvin had allowed several ballet companies to perform the work in the intervening years and had offered it to Todd. Alvin also agreed to arrive before we opened to lead the final rehearsals.

Alvin came to town to plan future residencies by his company (he and I made several fund-raising calls together to raise the money necessary to re-stage his work *Caverna Magica*) and to coach the Kansas City dancers in *The River*. He liked the dancers and they liked him. The ballet was a triumph and sold well even without the Girl Scouts.

Alvin's choreography fit the dancers beautifully and I thought the company looked magnificent in the work. He must have as well. Over the next few years, the company performed more works by Alvin than any company other than the Alvin Ailey American Dance Theater. This was not completely coincidental. The Ailey company had built a large and loyal audience in Kansas City. A group of local citizens, both black and white, believed that the Ailey company could help heal the rift between the two communities, and the Kansas City Friends of Alvin Ailey was formed. This remarkable group invites the Ailey company to Kansas City each year, supports new productions, and mounts educational programs. (They also created Ailey Camp, more of which later.) It is one of the most unusual and consistent support groups I have ever observed in my career. They worshiped Alvin and he repaid their adulation with a generosity of spirit that was awesome to behold.

While the Spring Program represented the happy end to the Kansas City Ballet's season, we had one more project to complete. In an effort to raise money, Todd and I had organized a special performance for early summer. We wanted to do something very special to mark the last performance before we changed the name of the company, to celebrate our new success, and to raise money for the following season. We decided to invite great dancers from several major companies to perform in a gala concert along with the dancers from the Kansas City Ballet.

The program was truly spectacular. Martine van Hamel and Patrick

Bissell from ABT danced the White Swan pas de deux from *Swan Lake* and the *Sylvia* pas de deux. Evelyn Cisneros from the San Francisco Ballet and Mark Silver of the Royal Ballet danced the *Fille Mal Gardée* pas de deux and the *Sleeping Beauty* pas de deux. Sean Lavery and Kyra Nichols of the New York City Ballet danced the pas de deux from Jerome Robbins's *In G Major* and the *Tchaikovsky Pas de Deux*, and Donna Wood of the Ailey company danced *Cry*. The program was hosted by Judith Jamison, who read a script I had written, and Jacques d'Amboise, who mostly improvised. Judith stood backstage and cheered on Donna Wood as she performed *Cry*, a lengthy solo Alvin had originally created for Judith. It was a scene I was to see repeated many times in my later years with the Ailey company.

The evening was a great artistic success. My opening speech, which chronicled the company's newfound success both artistic and financial, was interrupted twice by spontaneous audience applause. (The video shows my shocked reaction; I simply did not know what to do.) The dancers were astonishing and the audience went home elated. I will never forget the euphoria. We had worked extremely hard to put the event together; I believed we had created a unique performance of true merit. It was a good way to end the season. (The gala was to be, in retrospect, a macabre affair. Sean Lavery was later diagnosed with a tumor on his spine and retired. Donna Wood retired soon after to become a marketing executive at Philip Morris. Patrick Bissell was to die the following year of a drug overdose.)

Unfortunately, the evening was not a success financially. The Kansas City community simply did not understand the wealth of talent that was going to be on stage. We failed in our marketing efforts to make the case, we charged too much for the tickets, and our board was less than helpful in selling seats. I had failed to engage them in this endeavor. We ended up selling many seats for less than we had hoped. The house was full but the coffers were not.

Despite the gala's "failure," however, it soon became apparent that we had, indeed, paid off the entire accumulated deficit in one year. This was great news and marked an important moment in the company's history. But we were not yet out of the woods. Having no deficit is not the same thing as having reserves upon which to fall back or having a surplus for new investment.

But we were soon faced with this prospect when the National Arts Stabilization Fund (NASF) came to town. NASF was an offshoot of the Ford Foundation. Created by the dynamic Marcia Thompson, NASF aimed to help entire communities establish more healthy arts environments by providing the support, both consulting and financial, needed to establish stability. NASF was working in Boston and Seattle at the time and had entered into a partnership with the Hallmark people to do so in Kansas City.

The concept was highly attractive to all of us in the arts community, but we were concerned about the impact of this large program on the annual funding we all relied upon from Hallmark. The program was announced at a large press conference one summer Sunday. I can recall one less-than-interested city official watching the final round of the U.S. Open golf tournament on a palm-sized television as Marcia explained the program.

Each organization in the program would be required to meet a series of criteria set by the NASF before becoming eligible for funding. Once funding was offered, the organization would have one fiscal year to eliminate half of its net current liabilities position (current liabilities less current assets). If it accomplished this task, it would receive a grant equal to the remaining half of the net current position. If the organization maintained balance for four more years, it would receive a second substantial grant for endowment or a cash reserve. It all made sense to me.

The problems, however, only emerged over time. Hallmark, contrary to its promise, did suspend annual funding of the arts organizations included. You can imagine our horror at losing our major annual funder just as we established fiscal equilibrium. I was livid and complained to the NASF staff. But I soon learned I had made a major tactical mistake. The criteria one had to achieve before being offered initial funding were never specified. "The consultant will know when the time is right," we were told. By complaining about the loss of Hallmark funding, I had demonstrated that I was not fully supportive of the program, and this indicated that we were not ready for funding. I reminded the NASF consultant, Len Vignola, that we had paid off the entire accumulated deficit in one year. Did this not indicate that we were serious about stabilization and were ready for funding? "No," said the NASF. We had completed our strategic plan too quickly, we were told. Unless we made a new plan (regardless of the fact that the old one was working quite well, thank you) we would not be funded. And, by the way, I had complained about the lack of board support for the gala; unless the board demonstrated more support, we would not be funded.

In other words, we had to pretend that all was well before we could be funded. I came to believe that mixing grants making with consulting was counterproductive. One wants to tell a consultant everything, warts and all, in order to get assistance. Yet funders want to feel comfortable about the organization. When you are fighting for a company's economic survival, the pressure to ingratiate yourself with funders always wins and the consultative process becomes a sham. As presented to me at that time, the NASF program did not make sense. (The NASF people were not simply unhappy with me. Despite three more years of balanced budgets during the tenure of my successor, the company was still not funded. In fact, NASF funding only materialized nine years later!)

But I was not going to stick around to play this game. I had come to realize that I had done all I could do in Kansas City, and I wanted to return home to the East Coast. I also wanted to work in a larger organization. So I announced my resignation to the board and to Todd and suggested that they name Claudette Donlon my successor. Fortunately they took this suggestion and Claudette ran the company brilliantly for three years. Claudette had different ideas about the potential of the NASF program and was more of a team player. In fact, after leaving the State Ballet of Missouri she went to work for NASF in New York.

As I prepared to leave Kansas City, I was given the opportunity by Todd to play the Grandfather in *Nutcracker*. It was a wonderful experience to perform with my great friends, the dancers. Over the year and a half I lived in Kansas City, I had formed deep friendships with many of them that survive to this day.

I said a final good-bye to my staff and dancers on the tour to New York that had done so much to transform the image of the company. I traveled with the company to New York and stayed behind after they left. I felt as if I had lost my family.

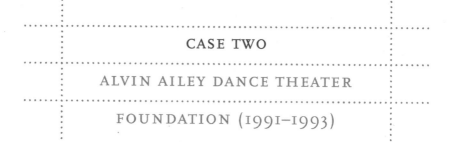

CASE TWO

ALVIN AILEY DANCE THEATER

FOUNDATION (1991–1993)

In September of 1990, after a stint at the Pierpont Morgan Library, I was approached about the possibility of running the Alvin Ailey American Dance Theater. I had collaborated with Alvin in Kansas City and was a huge fan of his work. Alvin had died nine months earlier at a tragically young age. The company, under the new artistic director, Judith Jamison, was in deep distress. While the artistic product was still strong (and, with Judith's energy, getting stronger after a period of decline during Alvin's illness), the financial situation was dire. The company had a deficit of more than $1.5 million and was suffering from the typical effects of cash shortages: missed payrolls, low morale, and ineffective fund-raising. The situation was similar to the Kansas City Ballet's when I arrived there although on a much larger scale.

Phil Laskawy, a senior executive of Ernst & Young and a longtime Ailey board member, met me while I was consulting to the Jewish Museum. He was certain I was the right person for the job. He asked me to meet with Ken Brody, a member of the board and a Goldman Sachs partner. Ken had the potential to make a major financial contribution, but he was an outspoken critic of the current management of the organization and was eager to make a change. Ken liked me instantly, so instantly, in fact, that he offered me the job during our first meeting. I was a bit surprised that he had the authority to make me an offer without my first seeing any other board members or Judith, but I was flattered and excited nonetheless. He asked whether I could start work immediately; I assured him that I could.

I left our meeting as elated as I had ever been. I was finally going to enter the New York performing arts scene. It all seemed too good to be true. A few hours after my meeting, still walking on a cloud, I received a frantic call from Harold Levine, chairman of the board. We had met a few months earlier, when the possibility of my doing some consulting work for the Ailey organization had been raised. That discussion ended prematurely when it was decided that there were no funds for a consultant. (I had offered to defer my billing, but the company did not want to incur any more debt, no matter how sympathetic the creditor.) Harold confirmed what I had feared: Ken had been a bit overenthusiastic and I would have to work through a proper search process. While I was disappointed, I did think that I would be a more effective executive director if the board and Judith were involved in the search process and did not feel my appointment was foisted upon them by one enthusiastic board member.

Once again I had to endure a difficult search process. I recognized that my resume in dance was very thin. All I had done was run the Kansas City Ballet for less than two years. One board member literally threw my resume back to Harold with the words "We can do better than this."

The theme of my interviews was, not surprisingly, how I could fix Ailey's financial problems. The company was deeply in debt and its very survival was in jeopardy. Huge sums were owed to numerous vendors and these vendors were getting very, very restless. I suggested that my reading of the Ailey financials indicated that the level of fund-raising was substantially too low. Ailey earned over 70 percent of its budget from ticket sales and tour fees and tuition to its school. This was one instance where statistics can be misleading. It is generally considered a good thing for an arts organization to earn a large portion of its budget since it indicates substantial public appeal and a degree of control over one's own future since the organization is not as reliant on contributed funds.

But the Ailey company was earning such a large proportion of its budget because its fund-raising was so inadequate. The largest modern dance ensemble in the world and the largest African-American cultural institution in the world was raising only $1.7 million a year. This was only twice what the much smaller Kansas City Ballet was raising when I arrived there. I knew the organization could do better and said so at my interviews. Many board members were skeptical. They felt that Ailey was raising all the money it could and that they simply had to close the school and the junior company to make ends meet.

I did not have all the facts but I knew they had to be wrong. After my stint at Kansas City, I began to develop my theories about the causes of problems in the arts. I realized that most organizations in trouble get that way because they react to an initial financial problem inappropriately. When any financial problem emerges, the first reaction of most boards and staff is to reduce expenditures. The easiest expenses to cut are the most discretionary areas of spending: artistic ventures and marketing. No one has to be fired to make these cutbacks. However, when arts organizations cancel artistic and marketing initiatives, they begin to lose the interest of their supporters, both donors and audience members. As a result, less revenue is received and further cutbacks are made. This begins a vicious spiral that cripples arts organizations. Where one cuts a budget is a crucial decision for any arts organization, and I believed Ailey was in danger of making a dangerous move if it closed its school and junior company.

My last, and most important, interview was with Judith. Judith had been running the Ailey company for almost a year. It had been a baptism of fire. While she had a firm idea of how she wanted the company to perform artistically, she had been buffeted by the tremendous financial problems and many of her artistic initiatives could not be implemented given the financial constraints. She was frustrated.

Ken Brody had done a good job of briefing her on my credentials and why he thought I was right for the job. In fact, Judith thought the board had already offered me the job and that her role in the "interview" was to convince me to accept. I, of course, assumed she had yet to make up her mind about me and I was anxious to impress her. The first half-hour of our discussion, therefore, was rather farcical. She was trying to entice me while I was trying to entice her. It was only after a bit of time that we realized what had happened and the resulting gales of laughter sealed a bond between us. I left her office feeling very good about the future.

By Thanksgiving, two months after Ken Brody had asked me to start work, I was finally offered the job. The board felt it would be better if I started after the company's New York season ended, on January 1, 1991. They believed that replacing the incumbent before the season would unsettle the company and the press. In retrospect, I would have preferred to have started earlier since once the offer had been made, Judith and others began to look to me for decisions.

Even before I started officially, I was involved in several Ailey activities that gave me some insight into the world I was entering. The first was the opening night gala for the company. The Ailey company mounts an annual one-month season in New York City, at City Center. The opening night of the season is always used as a fund-raising event for the organization. I was pleased to be invited to the event although I was concerned not to be too visible. My appointment had yet to be announced and I did not think it was fair to the outgoing executive director for me to "steal his show." He had been at Ailey for many years and had seen the company through good times and bad; he deserved his night.

The invitation for the gala included a long list of famous African-Americans who formed the honorary committee for the event, everyone from Michael Jordan to Bill Cosby. I was looking forward to meeting all of these luminaries and was excited about entering the first rank of arts organizations. In the event, not one member of the honorary committee appeared. I was disappointed, as I am sure were many of those who had paid up to one thousand dollars per ticket to attend. I decided then and there that I would never advertise luminaries who were not going to appear; it simply was not fair.

A few days after the gala, I learned that Ailey was to participate in an NASF program designed to support minority arts organizations in New York City. I was asked to attend a meeting, before I started work, to review the program and discuss key issues. I was skeptical at best. I had not had a wonderful experience with the NASF team in Kansas City and I knew that several years later, the Kansas City Ballet had still not received its funding. Moreover, the New York project was to be funded by the Lila Wallace–Reader's Digest Fund, a major supporter of the Ailey organization. Was this to be another instance of a major funder's withdrawing current support in favor of a longer-term gift?

At the meeting I was assured that this was not to be the case. Lila Wallace support would continue. My dear friend Claudette Donlon was a participant at the meeting. She had recently left the Kansas City Ballet and had joined NASF. It was strange to have one of my best friends on "the other side." She was totally professional, as always, and I do not think anyone else in the room was conscious of our friendship.

The meeting ended with our promise to provide all of the necessary documents to NASF to begin the consultation process. I, more than anyone in the room from Ailey, understood what a long road we were about to navigate.

The most troubling issue I faced prior to my joining Ailey centered on the salaries for our technical staff. I received a phone call from Judith just before Christmas asking me to see her backstage at City Center. When I arrived, she said that the crew demanded salary increases if they were to go on the forthcoming tour throughout the United States. They deserved the raises (the Ailey crew is the hardest-working group I have ever encountered), and she wanted me to get the board to approve the raises despite the wage freeze imposed as a response to the current fiscal crisis. She asked me to talk with Calvin Hunt, our production stage manager, who ran the crew. Calvin, a bear of a man, explained the problem of keeping crew at Ailey given the low salaries compared to those of other major arts organizations and the very intense workload. The forthcoming tour had a good deal of "one-nighters," one-day stops that were the hardest on the crew. He was not sure his crew would stay if salary increases were not given. I trusted his instincts, and I also believed that wage freezes were not the answer to cash problems.

Freezing wages was an approach I call "saving one's way to health," an approach I have yet to see work. I believe, rather, in marshalling resources, creating exciting new artistic ventures, marketing them aggressively, and using new funds to reinvest in additional important projects. It was a different approach than the board was taking but I did not see how they were going to reestablish fiscal health simply by holding salaries constant. (Many board members believed that the only answer for the company was for Bill Cosby to donate one million dollars. He had made it clear that he would give nothing until we had cleaned ourselves up, but they still hoped.)

I decided that the crew salary issue would be a test case. If the board leadership allowed me to give the raises, that would be fine. If they said no, then I had to question whether I would have the power I needed to effect change at this troubled organization. I spent a long Christmas weekend worrying about the impending battle. By the end of the four days I was convinced that I would never actually begin employment at the organization I had worked so hard to join.

When Tuesday morning arrived, I called Harold Levine and Ken Brody and explained the situation to them. They both said immediately,

You are the boss; do what you think is right. I was relieved and happily called both Calvin and Judith with the news. I was an instant hero with both of them and the entire crew, and that allowed me to start work in the best of fashions.

My first day of work, January 2, 1991, was one of those icy, stormy days in New York City. I needed to take my computer to the office (Ailey could not afford to buy me one), and I slipped and slid around the streets looking for a taxi. When I arrived, chilled to the bone, I was greeted by an emergency. We had been booked to go to Athens on tour in September. But our presenter at the Tivoli in Copenhagen thought he had been promised the same week. By coincidence his name was Mr. Kaiser. So my first act as executive director of Alvin Ailey was to call Mr. Kaiser and tell him that another Mr. Kaiser was canceling the Ailey tour to Copenhagen. He was livid and called me every name in the book (except Kaiser). It was an inauspicious first day at the office.

After my conversation with Mr. Kaiser, I met with my staff. As is typical in turnaround situations, they were quite suspicious of this new boss. What programs would I cut to balance the books? Was I a tool of the board? Who would be the first to go? Would I introduce my own team? Since, in my approach, my first impulse is to build programming rather than to slash budgets, I have ready, reassuring answers to these questions. I also do not bring in my friends but prefer to work with those who know the organization best. I am a planner and want my staff to feel they have input in the future direction of the organization. For most people this is an attractive environment in which to work. For a few it is more responsibility than they enjoy. This latter group rarely remains long.

After the crew salary victory, Judith, of course, was on my side and was a huge help. The relationship between the artistic director and executive director in any arts organization is immensely important. If the two work well together, if they trust each other's expertise, the organization is going to benefit. If there is mistrust, the organization is certain to fail. I believe that, contrary to conventional wisdom, the responsibility for most of the failures to establish a strong relationship between the two leaders falls with the executive.

Many people, especially board members with corporate backgrounds, are quick to point fingers at artistic leaders, who, they believe, do not understand fiscal realities. I, however, believe that many administrators take an arrogant attitude vis-à-vis their artistic partners and act like angry parents disciplining a spoiled child. In the end, the only important products of an arts organization are its artistic and educational programs, not the health of its balance sheet. Executives who spend all of their time saying what cannot be afforded rather than finding ways to achieve the visions of their artistic directors are not doing their jobs well.

My focus on increasing revenue, building the artistic program, and marketing more aggressively makes it easier for artistic leaders to trust me. When I fought for the crew salaries at Ailey, I was demonstrating to Judith, and the rest of the organization, that I was not going to try to "save our way to health." I believe that Judith would agree that my work was directed at helping her get done what she wanted.

Sometimes trust can result from a lucky coincidence. Judith walked into my office one day asking whether I could get the Ailey company on the Jumbotron, a huge television screen placed high atop Times Square. I explained that the Jumbotron was owned by Sony and we would have to get them to agree to put a film clip of the Ailey organization on the screen. I was not optimistic since the Jumbotron was used for advertising and I was certain that the cost would be immense. But I agreed to follow up. Literally ten minutes after Judith left my office the phone rang. It was the Department of Cultural Affairs for the City of New York asking whether we would be interested in having the Ailey company featured on the Jumbotron! Sony was donating time to the city and we were on the list to be contacted. I marched into Judith's office and told her of the coincidence. She thought I was being modest. In any event, we ended up on the Jumbotron every hour for a week. I will never know whether or not it had a marketing impact, but I do know it cemented my relationship with Judith.

One of Judith's dreams was to remount the Ailey work *The Mooche*. It was a very lavish ballet that required a huge investment in sets and costumes. It had been programmed and then cancelled the season before I joined Ailey. I promised Judith we would do it one day. But we had to wait. I have found that the best way to work with artistic directors is to let them name their priorities, and then propose a schedule for achieving them. The best artistic directors have a host of dreams; rarely can they all be achieved immediately. But I have yet to find an artistic director who takes the short-term view. This implies the need for a long-term planning horizon. Too many arts organizations plan only one year ahead. I typically work two to five years ahead, depending on the art form; this has many benefits, not the least of which is that it gives artistic directors the confidence that their important artistic priorities will be pursued in the foreseeable future.

But, to be honest, remounting *The Mooche* seemed a distant prospect at that time. It would be difficult to overstate the problems faced by the Ailey organization at the time of my arrival. There simply was no cash. We owed a great deal to vendors, especially the contractor who had recently refurbished the Ailey offices and studios. Our fund-raising effort was overly reliant on a few donors, yet these donors were rightly concerned that the company was always one step from bankruptcy. The board was tired and depressed and the dancers were angry.

In addition, Judith, who had returned to run the Ailey company, was frustrated. She had been running her own small company, the Jamison Project, which gave her the freedom to do what she wanted artistically within the constraints of the available resources. She had choreographed several works for the Jamison Project (my favorite was *Forgotten Time*, a rich, vibrant work set to the music of Les Mystères de Voix Bulgare) and had assembled a strong group of dancers.

Before Alvin died, he asked Judith to become the new artistic director of the Ailey company. Given her history with the organization and Alvin's role in her career, Judith could not refuse. In negotiating to engage Judith, the Ailey board agreed to hire several of her dancers and to pay off any outstanding debts that the Jamison Project had incurred. A year later, those debts had not been paid, and Judith felt that a promise had not been kept. She was also frustrated by the inability of the organization to meet her artistic needs. Who could blame her?

Judith was completely faithful to Alvin's vision for the company. He wanted his own works to be performed. But even from the very first performance by the Ailey company in 1958, he featured the work of other choreographers as well. Judith wanted to include Alvin's works, works by the choreographers whom he had commissioned, as well as ballets by many of the younger choreographers working in the 1990s. This all required money and we had none.

The Ailey company had always been a touring company. The company had a four-week season in New York but also toured the United States and the rest of the world each year. When I arrived, the company was set to embark upon a fifteen-week tour of the United States. Looking at the tour schedule, however, it appeared that several of the weeks lost money since the tour was not well planned. There were too many days without performances, long distances between engagements, and fees that were too low. While it was too late to affect this tour, I quickly went to work with our agent from Columbia Artists to change our strategy for future tours. This change resulted in substantial improvements in future tour earnings.

The Ailey company gave me my first opportunity to experience the touring life. My first trip was to Baltimore just three weeks after I joined the organization. I had my own room, traveled from New York to Baltimore by myself (the dancers and crew left earlier to rehearse), and ate meals by myself. I attended the very first performance of my tenure at Ailey in Baltimore. The performance was electric and the audience was ecstatic. This performance marked the beginning of a short-lived residence in Baltimore. The intention was to mimic the Kansas City relationship. But the motivating force in Maryland was its Arts Council rather than a diverse group of interested citizens, and the venture never really took off. After the show and a celebratory reception, I walked back to the hotel alone. Most of the dancers went out to dinner and to parties in small groups but I felt like an outsider. I hardly knew the dancers and was both awed by and frightened of them. In fact, the only time I had met the dancers before going to Baltimore was during the City Center season, before I officially started work. Judith introduced me after a matinee performance. I muttered a few bland words about how honored I felt to be working with them. I thought that I had not performed well, but after my remarks Renee Robinson, a senior dancer, came up to me and said, "You have a nice aura. You will do well here." I hoped she was right but circumstances were so dire I was skeptical.

Calvin invited me to spend some time on the road with the crew. He realized that I would become more sensitive to the needs of the crew if I saw what their lives were like. I also appreciated that going on tour was the only way to get to know the dancers. Since they only performed and rehearsed in New York for less than fifteen weeks each year, I would not really get to know them unless I did some traveling.

After feeling so lonely in Baltimore, I was pleased to accept Calvin's offer to tour with the crew. My first tour was to Washington State, where we performed in Seattle, Tacoma, and Yakima, a small town where Alvin's father was born.

The Ailey crew works incredibly hard. Their "normal" daily tour routine begins at the theater before 8 A.M. They meet the local stagehands, who will help set up and run the show but who typically have never seen the show. The trucks will have arrived overnight and the crew unloads the sets, costumes, lighting equipment, dance floor, and props as well as a personal case for each dancer. While the stage managers set up the dressing rooms and place signs throughout the backstage for the dancers (who arrive in the afternoon for rehearsal), the crew begins to set up all of the equipment. This is hard and heavy work. The local crew helps get all of the equipment in place, but the Ailey crew works diligently, quickly, and with great spirit directing and complementing their efforts. By late morning, the floor is laid, the sets are hung, the costumes are sorted and ready for steaming, and the lights are ready for focusing. During lunchtime, the sound man tries out his equipment for the first time. He has about twenty minutes of quiet time to get the balance right for the taped music.

After lunch, the final adjustments to lighting are made and the stage is readied for the dancers. They arrive for spacing rehearsals, and, if time allows, more extensive run-throughs of the show. After the rehearsal is a dinner break, then everyone prepares for the show. The show will last up to two and half hours, after which the entire stage machinery has to be dismantled and placed back in the trucks. When this is completed (usually by midnight), the weary Ailey crew loads into the crew bus (a "rock star" type bus with beds and a lounge), has a drink, watches a video, gets some sleep, and wakes up in the next city ready to do it all again. It is fun for a day or two; it is brutal for weeks on end.

But there are rewards. In the cities where we gave more than one performance, the crew had its days free and could enjoy sightseeing. The Ailey stage technicians see more of the world that way than any other performing arts crew. They also establish a camaraderie the likes of which I have never experienced anywhere else. This closeness was hard won. The crew was a remarkably diverse group linked only by their profession. Zorba, the costume mistress, was funny and eccentric and enjoyed traveling so much that she would go on holiday as soon as a tour was over; the rest only wanted to go home. David, our sound man, is still one of my best friends. We have virtually nothing in common except that we like each other. When my briefcase was stolen, David appeared the next day with a new one; it was typical of his kindness. EJ, our head carpenter, was the social director of the group; he was always up for fun. Dan and Phyllis, our electrician and stage manager, were married. They were more straitlaced than the rest of the gang. Neil, head of props, was the only Jew in the group. When we toured to Israel, Neil and I took a day trip to Jerusalem and visited the Wailing Wall together. Neither of us will ever forget that day or the bond it created between us.

The trip to Israel was typical of an Ailey tour. We opened in Tel Aviv at the Mann Auditorium. The Mann is a concert hall; we had to turn it into a dance theater in one day. We loaded in at night after a concert performance of *Aida* by the Israel Philharmonic conducted by Zubin Mehta. We stood in the wings, privately urging the maestro to seal the tomb so we could get started. Within twenty-four hours, the Mann looked like a theater with wings and proscenium arch, all created out of fabric. After a few very successful performances in Tel Aviv (the Israelis have always loved the Ailey company), we toured to Caesarea.

Caesarea is an ancient Roman amphitheater on the Mediterranean. While the ground is dusty and the changing rooms filled with spiders and dirt, the setting, at night, is magic. We did our usual one-day load-in and then had a lovely dinner in the town overlooking the sea. The show was fantastic. The stars in the deep blue sky, the beautiful Mediterranean backdrop, and the ancient setting seemed especially appropriate for Alvin's *Hidden Rites*, a series of pagan rituals.

We also performed in a small housing complex a few miles from the Lebanese border. On the bus drive from Tel Aviv, Nasha Thomas, one of our dancers, read my horoscope. It was not encouraging, predicting a calamity for me that very day. For once, a newspaper horoscope was entirely accurate. This performance was a disaster from start to finish. The "theater" was a platform in a park erected for the Bolshoi Ballet several weeks before. In the meantime, the oil in the wood of the platform had migrated to the stage surface and the entire stage was as slippery as a sheet of ice. Our dancers were not happy and refused to perform those works on the program that required large leaps and spins. We told the sponsor that the performance had to be shortened. When this was announced the crowd stormed the stage and we had to hide in the scorpion-infested basement that passed as a dressing room. Dan got sick and was vomiting so severely we sent him to the local hospital. When the dancers could be put into buses back to Tel Aviv, I was elected to wait until Dan returned from the hospital. I had no idea how I was going to get back to the hotel and spent a few scary hours dodging the poisonous spiders. Still, I would not have missed the Israel tour for anything.

We traveled to Tokyo, Copenhagen, Cologne, Boston, Seattle, Los Angeles, and on and on. All the tours were different but each tour was memorable in its own way. Performing in the Herod Atticus at the base of the Acropolis in Greece was special. Opening night was threatened by rain at this out-of-doors venue. Dozens of Greek women tried to dry the stage with rolls of toilet paper, quite a sight. When the performance was over, we celebrated in a Greek taverna. A host of Ailey crew and dancers drank wine, ate Greek delicacies, and sang show tunes. Even Judith joined in and gave renditions of the score of *The King and I* that she had performed in high school; only a warning from the local police broke up the party.

Tours to London and Paris were also memorable. We performed for two weeks in London at the Coliseum. The trip did not begin auspiciously. When we arrived, we found that an advertising campaign for the Ailey visit featured someone we did not know. It was an attractive black man, stripped to the waist and smiling. Who was he? We only found out the next day that the marketing director of the Coliseum had decided he didn't like our photos and hired a model. We all, especially Judith, were livid. But the engagement was a big success and the audiences went wild. A particular highlight for me was the company's performances of *The River* with live music.

The River was, of course, the Ailey work that the Kansas City Ballet had performed while I was there. Seeing the Ailey dancers do the work was interesting. Alvin had choreographed the work for ballet dancers, en pointe. The Ailey dancers performed in bare feet. The critics found this distressing. I found it different but not objectionable. There were a few moments when the line of the female corps, en pointe, was missed, but there were other moments when the remarkable modern dancers of the Ailey company brought something to the choreography that ballet dancers could not.

The Ailey company almost always performed to taped music, and hearing the London orchestra play the piece was a revelation. The Duke Ellington music was inspired and lush and diverse and we all were so excited at those performances.

Paris was even more special since we were performing in the Palais Garnier. We were awed by the grandeur of the theater, the Chagall ceiling, and the remarkable rehearsal studio backstage. The Garnier stage is raked; the floor slants so the audience has a better view. This is not uncommon in Europe but does not occur in the United States, where dancers are accustomed to performing on a level floor. On opening night, our first ballet was *Shards* by Donald Byrd. As the dancers performed the opening movement and raised their legs in unison, those of us offstage could see them sliding down to the front of the stage! But once again, the company came through and the audiences were ecstatic.

The most moving of all the tour dates I experienced at Ailey was not in a major world capital but in Opelika, Alabama. We performed in a high school auditorium. It was not an impressive building. But the audience was remarkably diverse, half black and half white. After the show, most of the audience (and the company and crew) headed to Denny's for ice cream and pie. The spirit of excitement and fellowship in the restaurant was remarkable. I have to believe that Alvin was smiling down upon us all and saying, "This is what I want my company to do."

At every tour stop, Ailey's seminal work, *Revelations*, was the audience favorite. And with good reason. *Revelations* uses deceptively simple movements and familiar spirituals to communicate a wide range of emotions and events. I saw literally hundreds of performances during my tenure at Ailey and have never tired of it. The dancers, and artistic leaders, of course, would hope that audiences were as enthusiastic about other works in the repertory. Alvin even tried to eliminate the work from an entire New York season but was not successful. Audiences love this ballet and demand it; I knew it sold tickets. We would sell about 50 percent more tickets to performances with *Revelations* than those without it. As we completed planning for each season, I would have an annual "negotiation" with Judith about the number of performances of *Revelations*. My guess is that these negotiations continue to this day.

While touring was at the heart of the company's activities, my work was primarily in New York City. As always, I initiated my tenure by developing a strategic plan with the board and the staff.

The planning process was not simple to implement. We started with a full-day board retreat to review the mission of the organization. It was a difficult meeting. Like many artistic directors, Judith had a very clear idea of what she wanted the company to be. Despite her tremendous skills as an orator, however, she was not comfortable putting her vision into words. She wanted the board to watch the stage and discern her intentions. They found this difficult. In the end, we all agreed to a mission statement, and I was charged with assembling a small committee to develop a plan to achieve this mission.

Using the same approach as at the Kansas City Ballet, I began by interviewing board members, staff, and artists. This was an enlightening process. In a troubled organization without any cash, everyone is frustrated. No one has the resources to do what he or she wants and too much time is wasted coveting the assets of other departments. I had to develop a plan that would demonstrate how all departments of the organization could work together to create new financial resources.

The Ailey plan focused on marketing and fund-raising. The high level of income already earned by ticket sales in New York and tour fees on the road suggested that our only option for increasing revenue was to build a substantially higher level of contributed funds. And I was sure it could be done. Judith was right: if you looked at the stage, you saw this amazing group of dancers thrilling audiences around the world every night. This had to be exploitable. We simply needed to get our message out and to organize a much more aggressive fund-raising effort.

While many, many people knew the name Ailey, they were not really clear about the merits of the organization and what it stood for. This fact became extremely clear to me when we received dozens of letters of condolence on the passing of Alex Haley, the author of *Roots*. Many members of the public thought Alex Haley and Alvin Ailey were one and the same person.

Building a strong institutional image takes time and focus and creativity and luck. We spent almost two years creating and initiating an institutional marketing plan. By the end of 1992, I thought we were ready to begin rolling it out. The events we mounted from December

1992 to December 1993 remain a textbook illustration of a meaningful institutional marketing effort.

In December 1992, the Ailey company was featured on a full episode of the *Phil Donahue Show*, at that time the premier daytime chat show. Phil Donahue and his staff created a remarkable opportunity for us. We worked for eighteen months with his producers to sell them on the concept: the dancers would perform excerpts from the repertory on the (very small) stage, and Judith would discuss her career and the importance of the Ailey company. Devoting a full hour to one performing arts group was most unusual for a ratings-conscious network.

The day of the taping was frenetic and exciting. The company had virtually no rehearsal time on the postage-stamp-sized stage and we did not even see Mr. Donahue until the taping so there was an electric feel to it all. Most members of the studio audience had never seen the company before and were enthralled. Judith sparkled. Phil was entranced. It was a magical event that was viewed by 18 million Americans. It was the largest audience ever to see the company. No other American dance company had ever had this kind of exposure. It started a buzz.

The month before the show was aired, Bill Clinton had been elected president for his first term. As soon as he was elected, I talked with Ken Brody, our board member who was closest to the Clinton campaign (and was to leave us to become president of the Export-Import Bank), about the inaugural gala. Could the Ailey company perform? He put me in touch with Rahm Emmanuel, who headed the inauguration committee, who got me to the gala producer. I made a complete nuisance of myself trying to get us on that show. Eventually my calls, faxes, videotape deliveries, and so on, paid off. The Ailey company was the only major performing arts group invited to perform at Clinton's inaugural gala in January 1993.

The performance was to be broadcast, with a two-hour tape delay, by CBS. I knew ratings would be high so I had the producing team promise (in writing) that we would appear on television. In the event this promise became quite important.

The two days in Washington, D.C., were memorable. Since the inaugural committee had limited funds and the expenses they were covering were small, we had to go "on the cheap." Judith drove Calvin and me down to Washington in her rented car. I sat in the back with all of the costumes and props for *Revelations* on my lap. You could barely see me through the stools, fans, and hats.

We stayed at a small, unimpressive motel since every hotel room in Washington was booked. The motel was near the arena where the gala would be held. Rehearsals were set for Sunday, a dress rehearsal for an invited audience (of twenty thousand) was scheduled on Monday, and the gala was on Tuesday. The performers included Michael Jackson, Barbra Streisand, Bill Cosby, Aretha Franklin, Fleetwood Mac, Warren Beatty, Michael Bolton, Goldie Hawn, Jack Lemmon, Sally Field, Judy Collins, and on, and on.

After the dress rehearsal, with an audience composed of people who had contributed to the Clinton campaign and had won seats by lottery, it was clear that the entire show could not be televised. It was simply too long. I went into high gear making sure that our contract was honored, that the Ailey company must appear on television. Ultimately the promise was kept and the Ailey dancers were viewed by 88 million people. But other performers, including an all-star jazz ensemble, were cut and the press howled.

On the evening of the performance, we were kept in an area adjacent to the door through which the Clintons would enter. Many celebrities arrived from Roseanne to President Carter. But Mr. and Mrs. Clinton were nowhere in sight. We waited and waited. The television people sweated; they had only a two-hour cushion between the live performance and the broadcast and they needed that time to make the cuts required.

The Clintons arrived more than an hour late and the program began. I stood a few feet behind the president-elect. The performance went brilliantly and I was so proud of my dancers. The Clintons seemed to enjoy the excerpts from *Revelations*. During the finale, with Fleetwood Mac singing "Don't Stop Thinking About Tomorrow," the Ailey dancers were up on stage with the entire gala cast. Several of my dancers wormed their way to stand beside the new president. In every press photo the Ailey dancers were front and center in their yellow *Revelations* costumes.

The impact on the organization, one month after the *Donahue* show, was huge. But we were not done. The previous year I had worked with the New York Public Library for the Performing Arts at Lincoln Center to mount an exhibition on the history of the Ailey company. The original reason for mounting the exhibition was simple: I wanted to have something to show donors in New York even when the company was on tour. We only performed for four weeks a year in New York, yet most of our contributors were local. What could I show donors that would impress them when we were not performing in New York? The New York Public Library for the Performing Arts has a rich and varied exhibition program; each major exhibition is developed with great care and mounted for several months. This seemed an ideal place to showcase the Ailey legacy.

Rob Marx, the director of the Library at that time, was very receptive to the proposal I sent to him in my first few weeks at Ailey. He asked me to meet with Barbara Stratyner, the curator of exhibitions. Barbara knows more about dance history than anyone I have ever met. She and I worked very well together on the Ailey exhibition, which we named "Body and Soul." Working on the exhibition became a passion. We uncovered many wonderful objects, photographs, costumes, and memorabilia that told the history of the Ailey company.

We took a tour of the Ailey warehouse in Yonkers and found a treasure trove. We found a box filled with Alvin's honorary degrees; it was a big bulging filing cabinet and was tangible proof of the esteem in which he was held. We had original costumes from *Blues Suite*, Alvin's first ballet for his company, and *Revelations*; photos of virtually every Ailey dancer and dance; costume sketches by Romare Bearden; and the single most interesting object, a tour scrapbook kept by an early Ailey dancer, Minnie Marshall, during an international tour in the 1960s. The scrapbook had pictures, programs, souvenirs, and even CIA briefing papers for the trip to Southeast Asia. It told so much about the roots and personality of this company.

"Body and Soul" was a big success and one of the highlights of my career. I will always remember taking Lula Cooper, Alvin's mother, to the exhibition. When she entered the room and saw his huge portrait hanging over the large exhibition gallery she burst into tears. A moment later she asked, "Where is my picture? There would be no Alvin Ailey without me!" Indeed Lula Cooper was right on several counts. Not only did she give birth to Alvin, she also owned his name and the rights to all of his ballets. We spent more than two years negotiating the purchase of these rights from her; the board and I believed the company should control Alvin's works. After protracted negotiations, we finally purchased the rights and the Alvin Ailey repertory will be preserved in perpetuity.

The opening night of the Ailey exhibition was preceded by an argument with Rob Marx. The library was opening another exhibition of costumes by Julie Taymor at the same time. Rob wanted this exhibition to be available to the opening night celebrants as well. I felt that the fantastic nature of these costumes might overshadow the humble Ailey artifacts. This was not a sign of insecurity; a central point of the Ailey show was to document the origins of the company. Eventually we compromised and the opening night was truly celebratory.

The Ailey exhibition was so strong that we organized a tour. The final stop was the Anacostia Branch of the Smithsonian Institution. So in March 1993, two months after the Clinton gala, "Body and Soul" opened in Washington, D.C.

In July of that year we gave a free performance in New York's Central Park. This performance, underwritten by Philip Morris, was a celebration of the sponsor's thirty-five years of giving to the arts and the thirty-fifth anniversary of the Ailey organization. It was a huge venture and not inexpensive. But I know that Philip Morris felt it got more than its money's worth from this project. I believe that many corporations do not enjoy the full impact of their arts sponsorship because they underwrite projects too small to attract press attention. A corporation that is willing to focus on fewer, larger projects can create far more visibility for their products and services. Over a two-year period, I worked with the Philip Morris staff to develop the Central Park event. In the end, more than thirty thousand people enjoyed this free performance and many, many more learned about it from the media coverage it received. CNN ran spots on the concert twenty-four times during the day of the event and the *New York Daily News* ran a full-page picture celebrating it.

The performance also gave us an opportunity to show our major donors that huge numbers of people, from all backgrounds, cared about the work we did. The crowd was so big we feared for the safety of those within the walls of Summerspace in Central Park. We had erected large screens outside these walls for the "overflow." People lined up for hours to see the performance and many thousands more were watching outside the walls. Yet you could hear a pin drop during Jawole Zollar's *Shelter*. It was astonishing.

In September of that year we received permission from the City of New York to change the name of West 61st Street, where our studios resided, to *Alvin Ailey Place*. The ceremony, when the new street sign was unveiled, was very moving. Even Judith cried.

In November 1993, two books on the Ailey organization were published. The first was Judith's autobiography, *Dancing Spirit*. Judith had worked on this book for more than a year with a co-author, Howard Kaplan. The volume was edited by Mrs. Jacqueline Onassis.

The second book was a series of photographs of the Ailey company taken by Jack Mitchell. Jack had a unique relationship with the Ailey company that spanned most of its thirty-five-year history. His photographs told the history of the company in pictures, echoing the exhibition Barbara and I had curated the year before.

The finale to this remarkable year was the opening night gala of our thirty-fifth-anniversary season. The performance featured the world premiere of Judith's wonderful ballet *Hymn*, which told the story of the Ailey dancers through their own words. Anna Deavere Smith, who had had great success in her one-woman shows, collaborated with Judith on this work. Both of them performed in the premiere; it was spectacular. The gala also featured a performance of *Revelations* with Al Jarreau, Dionne Warwick, and Jessye Norman as vocal soloists. Phylicia Rashaad narrated a film about Alvin, Maya Angelou read a poem in Alvin's honor, and the entire evening was hosted by Denzel Washington. It was a fitting climax to the thirty-fifth-anniversary celebrations and to my tenure at the company.

Each of the events described here was meaningful. Taken as a group, the *Donahue* show, the Clinton gala, the Smithsonian opening, the Central Park performance, the street naming, the books, and the anniversary gala, redefined the Ailey company as the hottest and sexiest dance organization of the time. This new institutional image helped the company to double its annual fund-raising from one year to the next, thereby meeting the requirements of the NASF challenge. By the middle of 1993, the company had completely erased its long-term deficit, without closing the school or the junior company, and was ready for a period of great health and vitality.

Too many arts institutions believe that strong fund-raising results from charming and professional fund-raisers. When the money does not flow, they blame the staff. The staff usually blames the board, wishing they had given more or had wealthier contacts. The truth is that the usual culprit is the absence of a dynamic marketing program that conveys the excitement of a thriving artistic program. After the high-visibility events of 1993 it was easy to fund-raise for the Ailey company.

As many other minority arts organizations do, Ailey received far more funding from foundations and government agencies than from individual donors. The exact opposite is true for mainstream Eurocentric arts organizations. Minority arts organizations typically serve audiences who have other giving priorities. However, I believed that the Ailey organization was an exception and that there was more money available from individuals. We developed Ailey Partners as a result. The concept was very simple. Donors who gave one thousand dollars as an annual contribution received a series of benefits. The extra attraction was that we promised to run a full-page *New York Times* advertisement when we reached one hundred Ailey Partners. The name of each partner would be included in the ad. We printed, on newsprint, a sample ad that showed how a donor's name would appear and included it with the solicitation package. Dozens of new or increased contributions were received within weeks of the mailing.

I believe Ailey Partners worked because the quid pro quo was so clear. This is essential in fund-raising. I have always observed that board members are happier selling gala tickets than raising unrestricted funds. Why? Because the transaction is so easy to explain. It feels less like begging to sell a gala ticket or table than to ask for money for operations since the donor is "purchasing" a clear benefit. In every organization I have run, I have tried to create programs like Ailey Partners where the "package" is clear, easy to explain, and presented in the form of an invitation. I have found board members much more willing to participate in this form of fund-raising.

The structure of the board was changing as well. One of the important conclusions of the strategic plan we completed shortly after I arrived was that the company needed a stronger board. Too many of the board members I inherited were lovely, supportive people who had a limited amount to contribute to the company. The growth of the Ailey organization necessitated a board overhaul, a painful but essential element in the organization's development.

When an organization is very small, board members frequently act like unpaid staff. They sew costumes, balance the books, drive people to the theater, and so on. As the company matures, and more staff is hired to fill these roles, the board is needed to provide resources and access to those with resources. Half of the Ailey board donated less than five hundred dollars per year to the organization when I arrived. This was simply not enough. The board voted to ask its members to make a minimal contribution of ten thousand dollars per year, although a few people who contributed in other ways were granted exceptions.

This new requirement caused many board members to resign. Several were angry and remain angry with me to this day. But the ability to draw in new board members, with both resources and an expectation that they are to contribute them, had a huge impact on the organization. And the strong marketing program we had implemented attracted many new board members. The vicious cycle endured by troubled arts organizations was stood on its ear; now people wanted to contribute to the Ailey organization.

We made changes to the way we managed our board as well. I believe that the staff leadership must market to its board members. If one only discusses cash flow problems at board meetings, one is not-so-subtly suggesting that cash flow is the measure of success for the organization. I believe we must discuss the true mission of the organization and the programs that the organization is pursuing to accomplish this mission at every board meeting. One must also celebrate successes with the board. When I started at Ailey, every board member was embarrassed about our problems and most withheld their support and the support of their friends; after the institutional marketing effort was initiated, and after we celebrated these successes with our board, their perception of the organization changed dramatically, as did their contribution levels.

Some of this change was the result of adding new board members, who injected new energy and enthusiasm. I added these new members in groups of two or three. I find that if one adds a single new member to an unproductive board, the new member is socialized to act as the others do very quickly. By giving a solid orientation to a *group* of new members, and encouraging their enthusiasm *before* they attended to their first board meeting, we helped to foster a new energy among all board members.

The one group that did not change at all was the artistic leadership of the organization. Judith reigned supreme, but she was supported by three invaluable aides. Masazumi Chaya, who had been promoted to associate artistic director shortly after I arrived, is one of the great unsung heroes of dance. Everyone calls him Chaya. Chaya was the associate artistic director of the company and maintained the quality of the performances. When choreographers created new works, Chaya learned every step. Chaya knew the strengths and weaknesses of the dancers and helped Judith cast each ballet. He was a delightful colleague and a true friend.

Sylvia Waters was, in many respects, the conscience of the Ailey company. Sylvia, a former Ailey dancer, had been very close to Alvin and was one of the executors of his estate. Through all of the negotiations with Mrs. Cooper on the purchase of the Ailey rights, Sylvia was a major force. She ran the Repertory Ensemble, the Ailey junior company, and was responsible, therefore, for grooming a generation of Ailey dancers. A huge majority of the Ailey company enters through the Repertory Ensemble (now named Ailey II). They all were schooled by Sylvia, as was I. Sylvia kept me calm and centered. She was the mother of the organization and I respected her tremendously.

Denise Jefferson was the Director of the Ailey school, the Alvin Ailey American Dance Center. The school was a large and important part of the organization. The Ailey dancers were unusual in the number of dance techniques they have to master to meet the needs of the many choreographers who work with the company, from ballet to jazz to many modern dance vocabularies. The Dance Center prepared dancers in each of these disciplines. Denise had to balance the needs of those advanced students who might become professional dancers with the hundreds of students whose interests were more avocational. To both children and adults, the Ailey school provided strong training.

Denise and I worked well together to ensure that the Ailey school could meet its educational goals while minimizing the financial support required. This included adding programs for young children, expanding our summer program, and establishing a joint venture with Fordham University. I was particularly interested in this joint venture. The students at the Fordham campus at Lincoln Center, across the street from the Ailey studios, could take Ailey classes to meet their physical education requirements. Fordham paid a fee for each of these students. Ailey dancers and students were allowed to take courses at Fordham as well. This two-way venture proved very successful for both organizations.

The Ailey school students gave performances throughout the year. These performances gave opportunities to young dancers to perform and to emerging choreographers to create works. Denise and I had a running "conversation" about the length of these performances, most of which were given in the school's semi-ventilated studios. The summer performances were particularly painful. Denise favored four-hour recitals where as many ballets were crammed in as possible. I preferred a shorter, more focused program. Eventually we always compromised. Denise's warmth and humor always made these discussions fun and we always ended up laughing.

The Ailey school gave me the opportunity to watch youngsters learn and develop the skill and artistry required of professional dancers. I remember how Amos Mechanic went from a gawky preteen to a beautiful dancer. Matthew Rushing, now an Ailey star, started in a summer program. There is a special joy in watching young artists mature; I hope one day to run a conservatory.

Judith, Chaya, Sylvia, and Denise composed the most coordinated artistic team I have ever worked with. They were all so dedicated to the vision of the company and provided an integrated approach to the training of the dancers. It was a privilege to support their work.

The dancers, too, were unbelievably dedicated to the Ailey vision. It was a joy to watch the senior dancers, Sarita Allen, Dudley Williams, Gary DeLoatch, and Marilyn Banks. Gary's illness and death were incredibly painful. The day he died we were performing on Long Island. The trip to the theater was the saddest I had ever experienced. The joys of touring were replaced with tears and introspection, but the memorial service we mounted at the Joyce Theater was filled with the exuberance and warmth that Gary brought into our lives.

Virtually every one of the dancers became a friend. I have always made a point of being a presence in the lives of my artists, taking time from meetings to watch them work. In every organization I have managed, I am a familiar sight standing stage right and exchanging words of support and commiseration. So much of the joy in my life has come from the friendship of my artists and the pride I take in watching them perform.

Dancers strive for perfection. All dancers. When they exit the stage they only dwell on their mistakes. I found that I could support them by being completely honest. If something was great I told them. If something was awful I placed it in perspective, but I was always honest and did not sugarcoat. There were so many Ailey dancers who were important to me. Many are still friends.

The Ailey dancers, crew, and artistic leaders gave me a great education in the lives of black Americans. I had been raised in a home where color distinctions were not important. But at Ailey white people were a minority and I learned a great deal about the issues and concerns of the black community. I gradually began to relax and to be honest about the differences between African-American and other cultures; this has given me the freedom to work in many other African-American organizations and helped me feel at home in later years in my work throughout the world.

Joining white and black people in this safe environment was a central part of Alvin Ailey's vision for his company. He was, perhaps, the inventor of the concept of outreach. He believed that his company had an obligation to take dance to the people, all people. He was doing lecture-demonstrations in inner-city schools in 1962, long before it was fashionable and government and foundation grants were available. He did it because it was right to do it.

Over the years, the Ailey dancers have become quite adept at introducing dance to children in the schools. When the Kansas City residency was established, some of the local citizens felt that an in-depth program was needed for local schoolchildren. The result of this belief is Ailey Camp, a summer program for "at risk" teens. The camp includes dance training in several disciplines (ballet, jazz, modern, etc.) but also includes personal development sessions and reading classes. The focus is on discipline and respect of body. These are central to the life of a dancer and especially important for children who face challenges of teen pregnancy, disease, and drug abuse.

Ailey Camp was well established in Kansas City by the time I started at Ailey, but we were able to introduce camps in Baltimore and New York. The New York Camp was mounted in cooperation with the Children's Aid Society. I worked with T Jewett, the society's head of fund-raising, on developing the program. During the initial camp session in New York,

I worked with the children on creating an Ailey exhibition. We used old photographs to tell the story of the Ailey company. It was a great success and much fun for me. One of the joys of working in the arts has always been the opportunity to work with children.

Another is working with important artists. The Ailey company attracted many choreographers of renown. Donald Byrd did several works for us, as did Louis Falco and Lar Lubovitch. Billy Wilson created a lovely ballet, *Winter in Lisbon*, to Dizzy Gillespie's music. The premiere of that work was given at an opening night gala in New York. Mr. Gillespie was meant to attend but was too ill to appear. Bill and Camille Cosby hosted the evening. I was especially pleased they participated because I remember his telling the organization that he would not be involved again until we had our house in order. I felt his appearance signaled a change in his perception of the company. A few days after the gala, a check from the Cosbys for fifty thousand dollars arrived; I was thrilled.

Another celebrity gala host was Jessye Norman. Miss Norman had a great system for supporting arts organizations. She would take friends to a performance and then make each of them write a check to the company. We always enjoyed those envelopes filled with checks.

Money, of course, is always a problem for an arts organization, even for one that is growing and doing well. Throughout the three years of my tenure at Ailey, we continued to work on the NASF program that had been introduced the month before I arrived at the company. If we were successful meeting its requirements, the NASF promised us $1 million, a huge amount for the Ailey organization. The money would be received over several years. The biggest and most important portion, approximately $400,000, would be received in 1993 if we were successful in earning a similar size surplus in that fiscal year.

The Ailey organization rarely broke even; earning a huge surplus would be an immense challenge. Making matters harder was the Lila Wallace Foundation's decision to suspend operating funding to all NASF participants. This was the second time that a major NASF funder cancelled its grants to participating organizations, and it made me furious. But, as I learned in Kansas City, since the timing of our NASF grant was purely at the discretion of the NASF staff, we could not complain openly.

Because I was so determined to meet the challenge and so scared that we might not, I spent many hours trying to figure out ways to get around the rigid NASF accounting. I had learned in business school that it is dangerous to use one sole accounting measure to evaluate success since there are always ways to make that one measure look good at the expense of true health. That was the problem with the NASF program. It only used one measure (current liabilities minus current assets) to determine fiscal health. I was certain there were ways to influence this measure by accounting "tricks" should we fail to earn the true surplus required.

I did not need to resort to tricks, however. As the 1992–93 fiscal year progressed, we realized that the impact of the exciting artistic and educational programming, board restructuring, marketing and fund-raising programs, and rationalized tours would result in the increase in funding needed to earn the NASF target surplus. It is one of the greatest sources of pride to me that we made that target and received our grant in an honest fashion. It had never seemed possible at the outset.

Our new fiscal health gave us increased artistic flexibility. For example, during the 1993 New York City Center season we restaged Alvin's *The Mooche*. The work, about three important black female entertainers, was not a great success. But I was pleased to be able to mount it since Judith had wanted to do it for many years. I had always promised that we would do *The Mooche* when we could afford to reconstruct the lavish sets and costumes. Having it on stage felt like a victory.

Another eagerly anticipated work of that season was Jerome Robbins's *New York Export: Opus Jazz*. This precursor to his legendary choreography for *West Side Story* gave us a chance to work with this dance genius. Mr. Robbins wrote to Judith just as plans to mount Martha Graham's *Diversion of Angels* had fallen through. He was interested in working with the Ailey dancers. (This also felt like a victory.) Judith and I met with him in his East Side townhouse and discussed his idea to remount this work originally created for the Joffrey Ballet.

I was pleased that Mr. Robbins was so positive. Our only encounter with him before this meeting occurred when I had first arrived at Ailey. Donald Byrd created an exciting new work, *Dance at the Gym*, which he wrote was "inspired by the choreography from West Side Story." Mr. Robbins had his lawyer write a stern letter of warning that no steps from Mr. Robbins could be quoted in another dance work.

In the event, Mr. Robbins did not need to worry. While the Byrd work took place in a gym, and may have been inspired by the *West Side Story* situation, there was nothing remotely similar in the two works.

Mr. Robbins was not pleased about producing *Opus Jazz* to taped music, but we explained both the financial realities and the requirement to tour. He relented but was not certain a tape existed of the music. We could not afford to make a recording so we followed every lead to find the music. I was determined to get Mr. Robbins working with our dancers. I thought they would learn from him, and I was eager to introduce the works of great choreographers to the company.

In this instance, this was a good idea that simply did not work. The ballet did not seem to "fit" on the Ailey dancers. In addition, Mr. Robbins insisted his work finish any program on which it appeared. It simply was not a closing ballet, at least not a closer in the Ailey mode. Ailey programs typically closed with a bang; this work was very cool. The work left the repertory all too quickly as a result.

As noted earlier, the 1993 City Center season opened with the wonderful thirty-fifth-anniversary gala and was hugely successful at the box office. A great deal of the success was the result of the ballet *Hymn*, which Judith created with Anna Deavere Smith. To market the season and the work, Judith asked Annie Liebovitz, the brilliant photographer, to photograph the ballet. Ms. Liebovitz was remarkably generous with her time. She took the dancers to a beach house and made a series of phenomenal photographs. They displayed the beauty of the dancers and the emotion of the work.

I felt they were a bit risqué and would lead to complaints from the more conservative members of the public, but I was overruled. I was wrong. While we had a few complaints ("You people should spend more time in church"), the ads and the photos were incredibly popular. One of the large posters we created still hangs in my den. The choice of photographs is very important. Most dance companies make a mistake when selecting photos for ads, brochures, and so forth. They select the photos that appeal most to the artists themselves. These photos may be beautiful, but they may not be enticing to the marginal ticket buyer. I believe the most dedicated audience members are going to go to a show anyway. We need to market to those potential ticket buyers who are selecting among several entertainment options.

I made that point to the Martha Graham Company when I did some consulting for them in later years. I love the pictures of Martha in Halston costumes. They remind me of the great works of that dance genius and the tremendously moving moments I have experienced in the audience. But I am going to buy my tickets anyway. I think the photos are not as enticing to the marginal buyer, and they do not convey the tremendous energy, joy, and diversity of the Graham repertory.

I have always favored pictures of dancers in movement, particularly male dancers, since women buy a larger portion of dance tickets for virtually every dance company. My first season at Ailey we had a fantastic photo of Desmond Richardson in our ads and brochures. We also, for the first time, advertised in subway stations. This drew a whole new audience to Ailey. I am convinced the dynamic photo of Desmond and its placement in the subways had an impact on our box office revenue, a record for the Ailey company. The Liebovitz photos had a similar impact. No one could look at those pictures and not be enticed.

By the end of the 1993 season I felt I had achieved at the Ailey company what I could. The organization had been transformed. I was exhausted, and I knew that I was simply not the right person to stay and take the company to a new level. Turnarounds take a huge investment in energy, emotion, and time. They are also incredibly scary. While it is fun and gratifying, in retrospect, to look at the steps one took to solve serious problems, when one is in the initial stages, it is very frightening.

One comes to work each day not certain whether one has the funds to survive until the next day. Making weekly payroll is especially difficult; one scrounges for the funds to ensure that the artists and staff continue working. Frequently, senior staff is not paid in a timely fashion. Vendors are on the phone constantly haranguing for money, and one has no good defense. They are owed the money. Smaller vendors and individuals, including choreographers and designers, are particularly in need of the money owed them. One feels guilty constantly even if one was not with the organization when the debts were incurred.

The staff and artists are demoralized by the anger they encounter from vendors, by the lack of resources, and by fear and exhaustion and uncertainty. They are in great need of leadership and support and encouragement.

If one is successful at creating the turnaround, the elation at the moment when everyone realizes the organization is in a different situation is intense and justifies all of the pain. But it leaves one exhausted and drained. One needs to recover. And the organization needs someone with the fresh energy and the vision to take the company to a new level. If one lived during the lean years, it is often difficult to loosen up and spend the newfound resources.

In December 1993 I needed to recover and I resigned from Ailey. It was painful. I had come to love the organization, its mission, my staff, and, especially, the dancers. I had found a home at Ailey and was continuously challenged and rewarded.

The dancers dedicated my final performance, the last in the City Center season, to me. I was deeply gratified and moved.

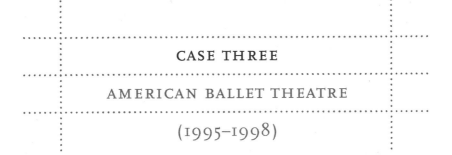

CASE THREE

AMERICAN BALLET THEATRE

(1995–1998)

After the rigors of running Ailey, I decided to renew myself by spending some time consulting to other arts organizations. I received a call shortly after I started my consulting business from Gary Dunning, the very talented executive director of American Ballet Theatre (ABT). He had recently been asked to take the helm of this troubled dance company along with the artistic director Kevin McKenzie. Gary had done a superb job running the Houston Ballet and Kevin had retired from dancing and had been associate artistic director of the Washington Ballet. In many ways Gary was the "golden boy" of dance management. He was smart, successful, and attractive and was hugely popular. He was chairman of Dance USA, the national dance organization, and had the respect of everyone.

I was deeply honored that Gary called me and was excited just to meet with him; consulting to ABT would be a dream come true. Gary explained the huge challenges facing ABT. There were similarities to Ailey: cash flow was a major problem and revenue had to be increased. There were substantial differences as well: while fund-raising could be improved, it was relatively strong. But ticket sales were not adequate for the New York season and touring activity was extremely weak.

This was not surprising. The collapse of dance touring had hit large ballet companies particularly hard. While many presenters could afford modern dance companies, with limited personnel and taped music, it was harder to pay large ballet companies and orchestras. When Ailey toured, we took about 45 people on the road; ABT traveled with 125. And the local presenter had to find and pay an orchestra. Its cost could be prohibitive. Yet ABT was founded in 1940 as a touring company; it could not survive on only eight weeks at the Metropolitan Opera House each spring.

The contract with the ABT dancers required the company to pay for thirty-six weeks of work, of which one was a vacation week. This meant that the company, in addition to eight weeks at the Met and twenty weeks of rehearsal, had to find seven other performing weeks each year. This was proving very difficult and the company was forced to cut deals that had it losing substantial sums on each tour week.

I felt, as I always do, that the central problem had to do with the nature of the art and the marketing of the product. ABT had always been the company of stars. The list of ABT principal dancers was a roster of the stars of ballet of the latter half of the twentieth century. From Alicia Alonzo to Erik Bruhn, Natalia Makarova to Mikhail Baryshnikov, Cynthia Gregory to Fernando Bujones, ABT was laden with celebrity dancers of the highest caliber. When Mikhail Baryshnikov became artistic director in 1980, he had a different vision. He wanted to improve the general level of dancing and aimed to build a corps of unparalleled excellence. He wanted to establish an ensemble and move away from star-driven casting. While he remained with the company, this policy worked because he was a star of such great magnitude. Donors and ticket buyers were eager to see Baryshnikov's company at work.

When he left in a dispute with the board in 1990, the company lost its greatest star. Although there were other dancers of renown and great ability, the company no longer had the long list of famous principal dancers that audiences were happy to pay to see and that donors wished to support.

As a result of the lack of "star power," ticket sales and contributions fell and the loss of tour income further damaged the company. By 1994, the organization was in dire need of cash.

As I always do, I started my work by interviewing staff and board members. I had a particularly interesting discussion with Kevin McKenzie, the artistic director of ABT. I asked him my standard questions: What would make you happy? What would you like to do?

Kevin gave me a long list of his ambitions: creating more new works, extending the New York season, securing more touring, engaging more guest choreographers, commissioning new music, hiring a music director, and so on.

I worked with Gary to write a plan that would help Kevin achieve these goals. The plan involved a huge increase in marketing and a focus on diversifying the repertoire. ABT had produced the same ballets over and over and audiences were getting tired of them. As a result, subscriptions to the Metropolitan Opera House season were falling.

Kevin had recently identified several young male dancers who he felt could have an immediate and immense impact on the organization. These dancers—Angel Corella, José Manuel Carreno, Vladimir Malakhov, and Maxim Belotserkovsky—were all distinctive and immensely talented. I believed we needed to focus our marketing on them.

Although I was working with Gary on developing these plans, I did not feel I was having any real impact on the organization. Gary would get caught up, quite naturally, in the immediate cash problems of the company. He was so busy trying to find the cash to make each weekly payroll that he had little time or energy remaining to develop longer-term sources of revenue. I am convinced that managers of troubled organizations must devote a portion of their time to implementing plans that will make the next year easier. Instead, too many spend so much time finding resources (and using up resources) for the short term that even if they survive the week, conditions get even more difficult. In other words, one must spend some time searching for new oil fields, not simply draining those one has already identified. This takes discipline and nerve; it is scary to spend any time working on plans for even the medium term when the wolf is at the door.

As matters got worse at ABT, Gary's relationship with his chairman, Peter T. Joseph, eroded. Peter was, by far, the largest contributor to ABT and a passionate spokesman for the company. He had strong opinions and believed his devotion and his contributions gave him the right to influence decision making.

Gary and Peter had hired an experienced consultant, Marcia Penn, to help restructure the board. Marcia had become a close friend of Peter's and was doing some work for his investment firm, Rosecliff. One Sunday night, I received a call from Marcia. She told me that Peter was desperate and she wanted my opinion about the steps needed to save the organization. I told her my ideas about artistic initiatives and marketing. I explained that the company was underinvesting in new repertory and it was hurting contributions, ticket sales, and touring. I discussed my approach to turning around arts organizations.

A few days later, Peter called. He asked me to meet with a few of the other ABT board members to see whether they approved of me as a replacement. I agreed and had a series of interviews with key board members. The truth is the board members were so concerned that anyone who entered as an optimistic leader was likely to meet with their approval; this is frequently the case with troubled arts organizations.

The board took the decision to make the management change and on Sunday evening, June 22, 1995, they met first with Kevin and then with Gary to explain their decision. Kevin was shaken; he was close to Gary and felt torn.

I met the next morning with Kevin and Peter to discuss an approach to informing the staff and dancers and to introducing me. This was a challenge. The staff was very loyal to Gary and mistrustful of Peter. I was to enter the following day and begin work. Because of the financial situation, some of the staff was already on a layoff (unpaid) period and the entire staff was to be laid off the next Monday for just one week.

I had one great ally on staff. Claudette Donlon, my associate at the Kansas City Ballet, was the finance director at ABT. She had started six months earlier when I recommended her to Gary. Claudette was, of course, a great friend and supporter, but she was in an awkward position.

The challenges she faced only increased. The last set of financial forecasts issued for the fiscal year (that was set to end the following month) suggested a small operating deficit of less than $100,000. Peter Joseph was determined to eliminate that deficit so that the company could claim that it had turned the corner and was operating with a balanced budget; after several years of deficits, this seemed extremely advantageous to fund-raising and board solicitation strategies. He asked Claudette and me to study the books to determine how we could eliminate the deficit. He also suggested he would convert some loans he had made to contributions if we needed a bit extra to accomplish this goal.

Claudette and I sat down together with the accounts, and it immediately became evident to us that the deficit for the year was more likely to be over $500,000! The development staff had made some very optimistic assumptions about the contributions we would receive in August, usually a quiet month for contributed income. More troubling were the cash flow implications of this new forecast. With the dancers due back for rehearsal and a short tour in September, we were facing an immediate cash shortfall of $700,000 for that month alone, in addition to the millions of dollars we owed to vendors. There was no way we would ever be able to survive this additional cash drain. And there was no point calling the dancers back from break and then having them leave when we could not pay them. Either we closed now or we found extra cash, and quickly.

I immediately called Peter and told him the bad news. I suggested that we consider closing the company for three to six months to evaluate how we could move forward and address this cash shortfall. It was the first and only time I recommended this drastic step, but I knew that we were in truly dire shape. Peter said that he would personally guarantee the extra $700,000. I explained that this was in addition to the contributions we "expected" from him, about $1 million for the year. He said simply and emphatically, "There is no way I am going to close the company; I will get you the money."

I gave Claudette the good news and she carried on managing the daily stream of calls asking for payment on past due invoices. One vendor, a small shoe manufacturer, camped out in my office and said he would not leave until I paid him. He told me his wife and children were hungry. That made our debts appear much more immediate and dangerous than I had ever experienced before. I wrote a personal check for our debt to him. A "friend" from a ballet-clothing supplier sent me a fax to welcome me to ABT and attached her unpaid invoices. We had run out of toe shoes and no manufacturer would give us more on credit. We had no Xerox paper. We took out every second light bulb to save on electricity. Welcome to the glamorous world of the arts.

Once again I was in turnaround mode.

I moved into my office and got to work. As always, I started by working on a plan and attempting to gain the confidence of the inner circle of donors, those who could really make a difference. But the mountain was just too high to climb. And cash was running short. Claudette, Larry Sterner (our general manager and Claudette's boss), and I spent hours each day reviewing our cash situation and deciding who would get paid and who would not.

I had agreed to forgo my salary for one year; we simply did not have the money. Several members of the senior staff agreed to hold their paychecks and did not cash them for weeks on end. But this was a mere drop in the bucket. We owed more than $5 million to vendors, as well as a substantial amount in back taxes.

Eventually we ran out of cash for even the most crucial payments and I had to call Peter for the first installment of the extra $700,000 he had pledged. Unfortunately, by this time, Peter, who had been diagnosed with cancer just before I arrived at ABT, had begun his chemotherapy and was not available to us. The dancers were back, the tour was going ahead, but we had no way to get the cash we needed. I had two alternatives: either I could lend the money personally to the organization or we could close down. I chose the former and made the first in a series of loans to ABT. (I had lent some money to Ailey during my time there but these amounts were small. The loans to ABT represented everything I owned.) I trusted that Peter would pay me back when he was healthier, but I was scared. I was running a bankrupt dance company with a very sick chairman, a pile of bills, an angry staff, and no personal safety net.

When Peter left the hospital he was eager to get back to work. He promised that he would repay me any money that I had loaned ABT if the company could not. He was moved by my loan and realized he had a partner who was as determined as he was to see the company regain its health.

I realized through my initial fund-raising solicitations with board members and other major donors that we would need to jump start our fund-raising effort if we were to raise the money needed to erase our deficit. We already had to raise more than $7 million a year just to break even. But breaking even was not good enough; we needed to raise substantially more to pay off the $5.5-million deficit.

I learned that there was one major stumbling block to our raising more money. Donors had lost confidence in our ability to manage ourselves. They feared that their gifts would go down a big black hole and would have no real impact. Even the several donors who gave us very large gifts, of $100,000 or more each year, knew that their donations were sucked up immediately by past debts and made no direct contribution to our future programming. While most donors remained loyal, some were dropping out or reducing their gifts and virtually none were willing to solicit their friends, the best way to build a fund-raising effort. We needed to inspire more confidence in our donors — and we had to do it quickly.

The quickest way to instill confidence is to find one or several people who will make major commitments even when matters look bleak. Peter was the logical choice. He was donating approximately $1 million a year to ABT and was lending additional funds as needed. He also paid for numerous dinners, events, and other expenses. His generosity was extraordinary. In fact, he was giving so much, so visibly, that some donors felt that their support was not needed. If I were to get a major gift from Peter, it had to be structured to encourage others to give.

Thus was born the Peter T. Joseph Challenge. I asked Peter to give us $4 million over the next four years, no more than he would normally give but a huge gift nonetheless. The gift would be made up of both contributions and forgiveness of the loans he had made. (Of course, I asked to receive the cash portion of the gift in the early years. Loan forgiveness would occur as we developed other sources of revenue.) The "catch" was that this would be a matching gift. Peter would only be obligated to give this money if we could raise an equal amount from new contributors or from additional gifts from existing donors. In other words, Peter's gift would be matched by new money, over and above the normal giving of our donor base.

I wrote an extensive proposal and faxed it to Marcia Penn, who knew Peter far better than I did. I asked her whether I should send him the proposal. She asked, "What have you got to lose?" I replied, "My job." She suggested the job wasn't worth much anyway. We laughed together.

I called Peter, told him I was sending over something for him to read, and said that he should think about it before firing me. I imagine he was suspecting another close-down plan. An hour later the phone rang and Peter simply said, "Let's make it five million dollars. Five million sounds better than four." I was startled and thrilled and am convinced to this day that Peter's immediate willingness to consider this plan rescued the company from certain closure.

Peter and I worked for several days on the details of the gift, including the recognition he would receive. We agreed that our offices and studios would be named the Peter T. Joseph Studios in perpetuity. I believe that Peter deserved no less.

This challenge grant gave me an immediate tool with which to approach every donor. It appeared to every prospect, when the grant was announced, that this money would save ABT and that their gifts, therefore, would not go down an endless hole. What they did not realize was that most of Peter's gift was part of our base annual fund-raising budget; their contributions paid off the deficit.

Peter had unrealistic expectations about the way his challenge would be met. He truly believed that the entire $5 million would be matched by extra gifts from our board members. I was a bit more skeptical. Many of them had given large gifts for years and did not appear to be willing to *increase* their gifts. In many cases just holding on to the historical level of giving was a serious challenge.

I actually did not want to meet the entire goal with board contributions. I wanted to use the challenge to generate grants from new donors. And we did in large numbers.

The most important of these was a grant from the Andrew W. Mellon Foundation. Anne Tatlock, a member of the ABT board, was also a member of the board of the Mellon Foundation. She had suggested that Kevin and I accompany her to a meeting with the foundation staff to discuss mutual areas of interest.

When we arrived, the foundation staff announced that they were interested in supporting us and had the impression from Anne that an endowment grant would be most helpful. I hope I did not let my disappointment show, but an endowment was *not* what we needed. We did not need cash to put in the bank. We needed cash for operations, for new productions, for rehearsals, for touring. We were not ready for an endowment gift where one can only spend the interest on the grant, not the principal.

I asked what level of gift they had in mind and $1 million was mentioned. I knew what $1 million would do for our cash situation and for the Peter T. Joseph Challenge. I suggested that maybe we could have a dual-purpose grant: part for new works and the remainder for endowment. They were receptive. I took the plunge and asked for $1 million for new works (over a three-year period) and $500,000 for an endowment grant. I asked for the new works gift up front and suggested that we should be required to match the endowment grant "three for one" so that we would be left with an endowment of $2 million, not a great deal but something to build upon.

They asked us to write a proposal to that effect and we left in jubilant spirits. In time the grant was approved and in March 1996, we received a check for $1 million from the Andrew W. Mellon Foundation.

It would be difficult to overestimate the importance of that grant to ABT. It meant that we now had the cash to pay off many of our crucial bills. It meant that we could afford to commission new ballets with some security. It meant that we could start to look toward the future rather than the past. I only regret I was not there to receive the check. I was with the company in Washington, D.C., preparing for our Kennedy Center opening, but my staff faxed a copy of the check to the Center so we could celebrate there. I felt from that moment that we had turned a corner and were on our way.

The donors who gave early and so generously had a historic impact on the company. While cash was still tight, we started to believe that, with time and a new strategy, we just might make it after all.

The new strategy was crucial. One of the mistakes made by organizations in trouble is to focus exclusively on paying off the debt. This is obviously the first step in getting healthy. But the world is littered with companies who were sick and raised extraordinary funds to pay off the debt but did not solve the problems that created the debt and fell back into the hole. I was determined that this would not happen at ABT.

The staff and I developed a comprehensive plan to ensure that we continued to build a healthy foundation. There were six key areas of focus in our plan:

- Touring
- New York City presence
- New repertory
- Education and training
- Marketing
- Fund-raising

TOURING

The dancers of American Ballet Theatre did not have enough performing opportunities. The year before I joined, between Metropolitan Opera seasons, there had been fewer than four other performing weeks. It was impossible to maintain the quality and morale of the company, let alone any semblance of fiscal stability, when the company would go for months without performing.

The central problem was that to stage a one-week engagement, a presenter would have to be willing to spend about one million dollars on fees to ABT, local stage crews, an orchestra, and marketing. Ticket sales could never cover this huge expenditure since most dance companies simply cannot sell enough tickets to cover this amount. If a presenting organization invests the large sums required for a full ballet company and orchestra, it needs to sell a great many tickets at high prices. Yet few ballet companies or dancers guarantee a sellout on tour these days.

When the number of presenters willing to take the risk of producing ballet began to decline in the early 1980s, American Ballet Theatre started to "self-produce" on the road. This meant the company would act without a local presenter and would bear all the costs and all the risks. While this put all touring activity in the control of management and would allow for extensive touring and performing opportunities, the losses were immense.

My analysis suggests that the central reasons for ABT's huge financial problems throughout the late 1980s and early 1990s were self-produced seasons in Los Angeles, Chicago, and several other cities. In London alone, ABT lost more than $500,000 on one tour and was forced to borrow enough to cover that loss from a very loyal patron, Howard Gilman. This debt mushroomed as the interest was left unpaid until after my arrival at ABT. By the time we completed payment on the principal and the interest, this tour cost ABT more than $750,000.

Clearly self-presentation was not affordable and we could not take the risks associated with this form of touring. But finding presenters willing to take the risk was most difficult. The Kennedy Center, which had once presented many weeks of ABT performances each year, had whittled us down to one week, at a fee that did not even cover our direct costs.

Unfortunately, covering our costs was not the standard by which we could evaluate a tour. We had guaranteed a number of weeks of work to our dancers in our union agreement. Every week of the guarantee we did not tour had to be a rehearsal week. A rehearsal week would cost approximately $300,000. If a tour lost less than that per week, it was a better financial deal than rehearsing. It was a depressing way of evaluating touring, but it was realistic. (Of course there was a minimal number of weeks of rehearsal needed to produce our performances, but achieving that minimum was never a problem.)

While I believed that touring should increase once our marketing efforts improved, I knew we could not wait for months and years to get it moving. Tours typically took one to two years to plan and negotiate so inactivity would have had an impact for years to come. Our union contract gave us the right to hire a portion of the company for a tour as long as the remainder of the company had its minimal weeks of work covered. I discussed with Kevin the notion of "half company" tours. We would take smaller ballets to cities that wanted ABT but could not afford the full fee. If the presenter could not afford an orchestra, we would perform to tape.

This was a very difficult concept for Kevin and the remainder of the artistic staff to consider. They knew we needed work. They were even willing to consider taking smaller groups of dancers as long as appropriate repertory was developed. But performing to tape was a sacrilege. Ballet dancers need to have a conductor who supports them, particularly when they are doing "technical" moves like turning or leaping. If one must end a pirouette or a grand jeté when a tape moves on, it hampers the quality of performance dramatically.

In the end, Kevin decided to try the tours and we booked a few weeks. We divided the company into two: Company A and Company 1 (there would be no place for comparison with these names). We performed to live music in some cities and to tape in others. Kansas City, Berkeley, Nashville, and even Benton Harbor, Michigan, got to see the wonderful ABT dancers. The dancers complained about the small towns and the taped music but at least they were dancing. Over time we found that the number of dancers on these tours kept increasing and that the losses on these tours equaled the losses on full company tours; at that point, the concept was dropped.

As with Ailey, touring was exciting but hard on the dancers and the organization. The dancers typically flew in to a city a day before opening, got acclimated to a new environment and frequently a new time zone, and prepared to dance to a world-class standard the next day. Hotels were not luxurious; we simply could not afford to stay in fancy places, particularly in larger cities. A visit was always made to a tour city before a tour was confirmed to find hotels that met the standards of the company; a union representative was always present on these advance trips, as were members of the technical staff who needed to evaluate the theaters.

The two most challenging tours during my tenure were those to Korea and Japan. On the trip to Japan many of our dancers became ill and it was questionable whether we would have enough swans for *Swan Lake*. Our Korean visit was marred by a truly awful hotel that reeked of kim-chi, fermented pickled vegetables that did not seem to leave us during our entire stay. Unfortunately these tours were not consecutive so we found ourselves going back and forth over the Pacific Ocean twice over a short interval.

The trip to Japan was preceded by performances of *Don Quixote* in Los Angeles, at the Dorothy Chandler Pavilion. The audience was so excited by Angel Corella and Paloma Herrera that they gave a standing ovation at the end of the Act 3 pas de deux. It was electrifying and we anticipated many return trips. I felt that this was one city in which we could establish a beachhead since Los Angeles had no substantial ballet company of its own. All of my efforts to build some permanent relationship in Los Angeles came to naught. The leadership of the Los Angeles Music Center, home of the Dorothy Chandler Pavilion, simply could not decide what kind of dance program it wanted.

Many tour dates, like the L.A. visit, were wonderful and hold great memories. Others are less pleasant to recall. The worst tour for me was our visit to a dance festival in Vienna. Vienna has always been one of my favorite cities, and I was delighted to take my dancers there. Our hotel was exceptionally modest, but clean and bright. In an effort to make a bit of money, the company had organized a "patron tour." This is not unusual in the arts. One organizes a tour for company patrons and sells tickets at a premium. The patrons have an opportunity to see the company on tour, to enjoy activities not available to normal tourists, and to support the organization. One hopes that the touring patrons will be so impressed that they will increase their support of the organization.

Unfortunately, the trip to Vienna did not enhance our reputation. The first night we had dinner in an Austrian castle with faded royalty who rented out their home to royalty-loving tourists. It was most depressing. The day trips were worse and included an interminable recital at a local dance school. The school, it turned out, wanted this group of "rich Americans" to come to its aid and contribute to improve its shabby surroundings. Nothing we saw that day encouraged anyone to be generous.

Worst of all was our "theater." While the great Vienna Staatsoper springs to mind when one mentions performances in Vienna, our programs were given in the royal barn. Literally. This was a modern dance festival that was not accustomed to hosting a major ballet company. The tiny stage barely held our dancers. There was no orchestra. We were performing in a barn. Our patrons, accustomed to the glamour of the Metropolitan Opera House, were not impressed. Nor were we. The patrons were lovely about the whole affair, but I was depressed; this was not the impression I had wanted to make.

To make matters worse, Peter Joseph was feeling terribly ill while enduring another battery of chemotherapy and had to leave a day after he arrived. This cast a pall over the entire trip, as did a dance injury. During rehearsals, Angel Corella was injured. Peter Marshall, our company physiotherapist, was terribly upset and was not sure that Angel would ever dance again. (He did, and brilliantly.) The entire trip was a disaster.

One factor that makes tours so difficult to book is the presenter's difficulty in selling tickets. Except in the rare instance when a company has achieved huge international prominence (e.g., Bolshoi or Kirov) or individual dancers are famous (e.g., Baryshnikov) dance companies tend to sell more tickets at home than on tour.

The reason is that the home audience knows the dancers and the repertory; many company fans will want to see all of the repertory and even see several dancers do the same role. I argued to presenters, therefore, that they needed to build more intensive relationships with the dance companies they presented. This could take the form of presenting longer seasons or mounting auxiliary events like master classes and lecture-demonstrations that allow an audience to get to know a company better. Ideally, a presenter would employ the same company annually. This would give local audiences a chance to get to know and appreciate the dancers.

I tried to introduce the concept of an annual residence while I was at ABT. ABT had visited both the Kennedy Center in Washington, D.C., and the Performing Arts Center in Orange County, California, virtually every year for many years. I added a relationship with the Michigan Opera Theatre in Detroit. We hoped to introduce activities that would build bridges to the local community. We were most successful in Detroit, where we added a summer camp and a series of master classes and other educational events. This program of events allowed me to help the local presenter raise funds to support our annual residence.

ABT also established a brief relationship with the new New Jersey Performing Arts Center (NJPAC). The opening night of NJPAC was a gala performance including many groups that would participate, including Ailey and ABT. It was wonderful to see two of "my" organizations present, though the Ailey performance far outshone the *Swan Lake* pas de deux that our poor ABT dancers had to dance in front of an orchestra on a stage the size of a postage stamp.

The ABT run of *Cinderella* was more successful, but it was marred by what I perceived as a lackluster marketing and fund-raising effort. The opening of NJPAC was rightfully a major news story and the halls filled in the first few weeks as people wanted to see the new Center. But it was clear to me that repeat success would demand a more sophisticated marketing effort than was employed. One simply cannot sell ballet, opera, symphonic music, jazz, theater, and comedy in the same brochure to the same audience.

It saddened me, but did not surprise me, when the relationship between ABT and NJPAC ended a few months after I left ABT. The difficulty of marketing dance cannot be overstated. While I am convinced that ABT and NJPAC should have a long-term relationship—much of ABT's Met season audience is from northern New Jersey—the marketing effort has to be focused, and intense. And, as has been patently clear everywhere that presenting dance is attempted, one has to find a dedicated corps of donors who care specifically about dance. I remain convinced that this will be the answer to dance touring; it will be the only way that enough funding can be generated to support visiting dance companies.

NEW YORK PRESENCE

While touring was a great concern, our presence in our home city had a far greater impact on our financial health.

The fund-raisers and marketers of American Ballet Theatre faced a very difficult challenge. The company was only visible in New York for eight weeks each year during its annual Metropolitan Opera season in May and June. Selling tickets to the Met season was a challenge since the public heard nothing from the company for months after the preceding season. Fund-raisers were also challenged to raise a great deal of money during these "empty" months. If one accepts the premise that it is easier to raise funds for a visible organization, then one can appreciate the problems at ABT.

I knew we had to do more to make ABT seem "at home" in New York City. It was amazing how many people, even those in New York, thought ABT was housed in Washington, D.C. This notion was based on the many years that ABT had long seasons at the Kennedy Center. But it signaled a problem with the image of the company.

We needed to act quickly; not long after I arrived we initiated two short-term projects. The first was a master class series at the Danny Kaye Playhouse. I knew that we could create an exciting program of celebrity master class teachers working with young company dancers. This would have the dual benefits of showcasing some of the glamorous dancers of the past and educating audiences about the technical, emotional, and theatrical elements of dancing.

Our first master class took place in December 1995. Cynthia Gregory taught three dancers from our junior company a solo from *Les Sylphides*. The audience, composed of members of our Friends group, arrived in high spirits. They were very happy to have ABT doing something between Met seasons.

It was a magical and successful evening. Cynthia was wonderful. She revealed the images she used as she was dancing and imparted many important stylistic and technical pointers to the young dancers. Many of the audience members went away feeling that they had a new understanding of ballet and the challenges facing dancers. Most important, they all believed that a new day was dawning for ABT. The Peter T. Joseph Challenge and the master class were the two most important public signs that conditions were changing at ABT.

But no single program can create a turnaround. The "half-life" of the impact of any event is quite short in our culturally dense world, particularly in New York City. I knew we had to do more. I contacted my old friend Barbara Stratyner at the New York Public Library for the Performing Arts at Lincoln Center. Creating the Ailey exhibition with Barbara had been such a good experience; would she do it again for American Ballet Theatre? The answer was yes—and no.

The library had done a big ABT exhibition for the fiftieth anniversary of the company in 1990. We had to find a topic that was more specific than simply the history of ABT. As I was mulling over this challenge from Barbara, I was also working on plans to establish a fall season in New York. Since touring was proving so hard to organize, we had to fill our guaranteed weeks of work to the dancers in some fashion. But where? A consistent concern raised about ABT was the lack of a home theater. The New York City Ballet had the State Theater, the Paris Opera Ballet had the Palais Garnier, the Royal Ballet had the Royal Opera House, and so forth. We were one of the few major international companies without our own theater.

I appreciated all the reasons for wanting a home theater, especially controlling one's own seasons and costs. But I also felt that there was a downside to owning a theater: one had no flexibility. The Metropolitan Opera House is a fantastic theater for full-length large-scale ballets. But it is not the ideal setting to see the more intimate works of Antony Tudor or Agnes de Mille. This smaller-scale repertory was central to the artistic mission of the company and to its history. But these works did not sell out the Met's four thousand seats as predictably as did the popular full-length story ballets. Since there was no possibility of obtaining our own theater in the foreseeable future, why not turn lemons into lemonade? Let's use two theaters.

I met with Judith Dakin at City Center and asked whether she would be receptive to housing a fall season by ABT. Of course she was; City Center had suffered as much as anyone from the decline in dance touring and was anxious to have more companies use its facilities. ABT had been born at City Center; this would be a homecoming.

Kevin, of course, was delighted with the concept of a two-week season (which we hoped would grow over time) in New York each autumn and was especially grateful for the opportunity to do the repertory that did not work as well, artistically or financially, at the Met.

There were obstacles to overcome. In particular, our contract with the Metropolitan Opera, which was about to expire, included a restriction on ABT's appearances in New York. Simply put, we were not allowed to perform in any other venue in New York City. Period. In a lengthy renegotiation with the Met, we obtained the right to do a fall season at City Center with a series of conditions regarding repertory and ticket pricing. The Met wanted to make sure that the prices of the two seasons bore some relationship to each other and that the repertory at the Met did not suffer because of investment in the fall season.

These were logical and reasonable requests. ABT rented the Met for eight weeks each year, paying not only a rental fee but also all the costs of stagehands, box office personnel, and front-of-house personnel for these two months each year. This income was extremely helpful to the Met. The management of the Met had seen ABT suffer in recent years and was concerned that we not overextend ourselves and jeopardize our ability to mount a successful season in their theater. I managed to convince the general manager of the Met, Joe Volpe, that City Center would help the Met season by keeping ABT in the public eye and would not cannibalize our seasons at the Met.

Joe appreciated that City Center would give us a more intimate space and a more economic one in which to showcase the smaller works of our repertory; he was just as happy to have ABT focus on the full-length ballets at the Met. Kevin and I discussed themes for the first City Center season. Since he hoped that the City Center season would house many new repertory works, and since so many important works in our history had been created for City Center (before ABT moved to the Met), I suggested we focus the first City Center season on works that had been created for ABT. This would highlight the creativity that had been encouraged by the organization and suggest the crucial role ABT had played in American dance history.

As we discussed this possibility, it occurred that we now had a theme for our exhibition at the Public Library as well. Why not mount an exhibition about works created by ABT over its history? Barbara thought it was a great idea and liked the tie-in to the City Center season.

NEW REPERTORY

The initial City Center season and the exhibition at the New York Public Library for the Performing Arts would reveal the rich vein of ballets that had been created for American Ballet Theatre, from Balanchine's *Theme and Variations* to Robbins's *Fancy Free* to De Mille's *Fall River Legend* to Tudor to Taylor to Tharp. Many great choreographers had created many great works for ABT. But the company's weakened financial condition matched by a huge increase in the cost of mounting new works had reduced substantially its ability to commission new ballets.

Yet dance audiences want, and expect, to see new works. Much more so than audiences in the concert hall or the opera house, dance audiences like to see new works and to see the art form develop. Perhaps this relates to the relatively short history of concert dance. But whatever the reason, it is interesting to note that many important twentieth-century musical compositions were created for ballet; the hunger for new dance works inspired many important composers to create their greatest works.

Like virtually all artistic directors, Kevin wanted to commission new works for his dancers. I knew I had a responsibility to find him the resources to do so. One of the best works created for ABT during my tenure was *Without Words* by Nacho Duato. Nacho had already created *Remanso*, a powerful trio for men, for the company. *Without Words*, for my last City Center season, to music by Schubert, had four lovely pas de deux and was an instant audience hit. (It did not fare so well with Clement Crisp, a dean of British critics. Clement, a good friend, disliked Jiri Kylian and anyone associated with him, including Nacho. When ABT performed *Without Words* on a Paris tour, he wrote that the title should be *Unspeakable!*) Twyla Tharp created *The Elements*, a dynamic work to French music, for my first Met season and *Known by Heart*, a powerful work, for my second City Center season. In the process, I became one of Twyla's greatest admirers.

These works were all one-act ballets included in repertory evenings featuring three or more works. One of the factors working against the commissioning of new ballets is that the audience for "triple bills" is substantially smaller than for full-length story ballets. American Ballet Theatre, like most major ballet companies, struggles to sell tickets to triple bills. *Nutcracker, Swan Lake, Giselle,* and so on are far easier to sell. While dance enthusiasts will happily go to repertory evenings, the casual ballet goer is more comfortable purchasing tickets for a ballet that is familiar.

This is especially true for *Nutcracker*. It is safe to say that many regional ballet companies can only produce triple bills because of the money made each Christmastime through multiple performances of *Nutcracker*. ABT's main "rival," the New York City Ballet, is no exception. Were it not for several weeks of *Nutcracker* performances, the company could not afford the remainder of its season. This Christmas classic is so lucrative not only because tickets sell in large numbers, but also because the advertising expenditures required to sell tickets are so minimal. I have always differentiated between what I term "informational marketing" and "missionary marketing." The former is the kind of marketing one does for *Nutcracker*. All one has to do is tell people that it is time to buy their *Nutcracker* tickets, mention where to call, and list the performance dates. There is little other information needed to sell these performances.

Missionary marketing is far more complicated. In a missionary marketing effort one must convince people that they will enjoy a ballet even if they have never heard of it. It requires communicating much more information through words and images. It is much harder, more expensive, and less productive. It is important to understand whether a project requires informational marketing or missionary marketing because the difference between them affects the marketing campaign dramatically.

Nutcracker is so important because one can sell so many performances and need simply to pursue a widespread informational marketing program; simple direct mail augmented with print and radio advertising, email, and posters are all that are required.

Unfortunately, ABT has no *Nutcracker* season in New York; the Metropolitan Opera is at the height of its season in December and would not cede the hall to ABT at holiday time. Therefore ABT cannot benefit from the relatively easy sell of *Nutcracker*. ABT must compensate for the lack of a *Nutcracker* season by producing many full-length ballets during its Metropolitan Opera season. Many critics chastised ABT for performing so many full-length ballets, but these same critics never found fault with other ballet companies for mounting *Nutcracker* performances for weeks on end.

While ABT needed to produce the major story ballets, there was a constant desire to find new ones. *Sleeping Beauty, Swan Lake, Giselle* would routinely sell out easily. *La Bayadere* and *Romeo and Juliet* would also fare well. Less successful was *Coppelia*, and *Manon* was a disaster in New York during my tenure. The list of existing full-length productions was a short one and Kevin and I kept looking for new ideas. Before I arrived at ABT, Lar Lubovitch had proposed that he create a full-length ballet based on the play *Othello*. He had an idea for the work that would make it relatively low cost for a full-length production but would tell the story faithfully. The key to a good story ballet is to select a story that can be told in pictures. One can easily draw a "storyboard" for the great full-length ballets—*Nutcracker, Swan Lake, Giselle*. However, it is difficult to convey the nuance of conversation in dance. *Hamlet*, for instance, would be a challenging ballet to stage. *Othello*, however, has a far simpler plot.

Lar's idea seemed a strong one and I believed that mounting a new full-length ballet would make a statement. In fact, since Lar wanted to commission a new score, it would mark the first time in the entire history of ABT that the company would commission a full-length ballet to a new score. We announced the project well before its premiere. This allowed us to benefit from the anticipation and the impression this large project made while having the time to find the funding.

The creation of *Othello* was one of the most interesting and exciting group efforts I have experienced. Lar clearly took the lead; it was his project. But he needed a dedicated team to help. Lar knew of a young composer, Elliot Goldenthal, whose music Lar enjoyed. Elliot and his partner, Julie Taymor, had recently written a musical that had been nominated for a Tony Award. Julie, of course, was busy on a new project, *The Lion King*. Elliot had written an interesting symphonic/choral work that had had a big success on the West Coast. He was excited by Lar's vision for *Othello* and agreed to compose the score. Claudette and I eventually reached an agreement on contract terms. We did not have the means to pay a normal fee and Elliot was extremely generous with us.

Lar's original idea had been for very minimal sets. He had anticipated a window, a door, and so forth—simple pieces to convey each location. His search for a set designer led him to George Tsypin, a Russian designer living in the United States. George brought in his portfolio, primarily of opera designs. They were original, modern, fantastic. It was not clear immediately how they would translate to ballet since the floor has to be clear for dancing, nor how we could afford to build his sets. He was so excited by the project he promised he would find inexpensive ways to meet the needs of the work.

Lar also wanted to use Ann Hould-Ward as costume designer. Ann was a top theater designer who had recently won a Tony Award for *Beauty and the Beast*. She is a delightful person and colleague and we were all thrilled to have her join the project.

What was clear to everyone was that we had assembled, thanks to Lar, a stellar team that was going to create a very interesting work. But it was also clear that this work was going to cost far more than we had anticipated and that the team deserved to be given a budget that would allow it to do its best work. I believed we could raise a substantial sum for *Othello*, but I was frightened of carrying the budget alone.

I asked Kevin whether he would mind if we shared *Othello* with another ballet company. We would only do the work a few times a year, at best, and it was a shame to create such a large work and keep it in the warehouse. Like opera companies, we had the opportunity to find a co-producer. Kevin was completely open to the idea. So was Lar. Finding another company to co-produce the work would mean his work would be more widely seen; he could also have a larger initial budget to play with.

Kevin called many of his fellow artistic directors. Several expressed interest, but only one, Helgi Thomasson at San Francisco Ballet, had money to spend and the desire to participate. All at once, we could increase the project budget while reducing the amount invested by ABT, a "win-win" scenario.

By the time all of the creative artists were contracted and work had begun, we did not have a great deal of time to create the ballet: less than nine months. For a new full-length ballet, with a new score, this was no time at all.

Lar had already created his "libretto," the story he planned to tell, so it was up to Elliot to write the score, George to create the sets, and Ann to create the costumes. As Elliot was writing, we would hear snippets brought to us by Lar. In this day of the synthesizer, it is so much easier to write music and, especially, to provide a tape for rehearsals while the actual scoring is completed and each orchestral part is written.

Elliot's music was exciting and vibrant. Lar was particularly pleased with it and felt that he had the material to create his dance. George stepped forward with his proposed design: a series of glasslike panels that would move across the stage as large pictures were projected at the rear of the stage. The "glass" panels had embedded patterns that made them look like the kuba clothes, woven fabrics with geometric patterns, that were sold at all of the South African flea markets. They recalled Othello's African roots and were quite beautiful. We were all very pleased with the designs although a bit scared about the weight and mobility of the panels.

Ann presented a host of costume designs. They were meant to show the movement of the legs of the dancers through diaphanous cloth that created period costumes. We loved them on sight.

Everything was moving along well and we all felt we were creating something important. Now Lar had to choreograph. When we discussed casting, both Lar and I had suggested engaging the same dancer to play Othello: Desmond Richardson. Desmond, who had been such an important part of the Ailey company when I was there, had recently left the Frankfurt Ballet, where he danced for William Forsythe. Desmond is a strong, muscular, beautiful dancer who would be perfect for Lar's choreography. Kevin agreed and Desmond was engaged.

His Desdemona was Sandy Brown, an ABT soloist who had performed in Kenneth MacMillan's last work, the climactic pas de deux in *Carousel*, at the Vivian Beaumont Theater. Lar always enjoyed working with her and she was lovely.

Before Desmond was available to start rehearsing, Lar worked with Keith Roberts, an ABT dancer who was every choreographer's dream. Keith is smart and remembers every step as soon as it is created. Othello was created on him, as was Cassio, the role Keith danced in the world premiere. He also danced Othello in some performances in that first run, with a wonderful Julie Kent as Desdemona.

The role of Iago, obviously pivotal, was given to Robert Hill, a senior ABT dancer. He was remarkable in the role. Susan Jaffe danced his wife, Emilia. It was a dream cast.

As we moved toward opening night, matters got tense. Our Met schedule did not allow for enough stage rehearsal, especially with an orchestra. Remember that *Othello* was only one of seven full-length ballets performed in an eight-week season at the Met. I approved an extra expenditure so our orchestra could learn the challenging music, but we simply had too few stage rehearsals. The set was large and dramatic but scary to operate with panels moving during the scenes. The rear projections, designed by Wendell Harrington, seemed foolproof until one performance, when the machine broke down and the slides ran out of sequence, leading to some unusual images.

To pay for all of this we had embarked on a major fund-raising drive that involved many donors. The lead contribution was the Andrew W. Mellon Foundation grant from the year earlier. Other funders included a group of corporations and individuals who each gave fifty thousand dollars to sponsor the project.

The opening night of *Othello* was incredibly exciting. We had a dinner before the performance for all of the funders. While we were nervous about the stage technology, we were so pleased with the work that we were all very jovial. Opening nights can be dismal when you know the work is awful and you have to put a brave face on it for the critics, donors, and the public. No such effort was required for *Othello*. We knew we had created a major work; whether the critics and audience liked it was another matter.

The opening performance was beautiful, the dancers were superb, the sets worked, and the audience was responsive. There were quibbles. The first act did not have much dancing, but most story ballets have first acts that are primarily exposition. Desdemona's dress was not becoming and was changed for future productions. But in general the audience response was strong. We had done so much talking about the production that we sold a remarkable 90 percent of the tickets at the Met, equating to more than thirty-five hundred seats per performance, a huge number for a new work.

The critics were divided. No one called it a masterpiece. Anna Kisselgoff, writing in the *New York Times*, was very supportive; Clive Barnes in the *New York Post* was not: "Moor or Less a Disaster" read the headline. But the audiences kept coming and we were exceptionally proud.

While *Othello* was by the far the largest artistic venture during my three years at ABT, it was certainly not the only one. In collaboration with the Houston Ballet, we co-produced another new full-length ballet, *The Snow Maiden*, to music by Tchaikovsky and choreography by Ben Stevenson, the artistic director of the Houston Ballet. *The Snow Maiden* is a classic Russian fairy tale. Ben created a lovely, if overlong, production with elaborate sets and costumes by Desmond Heeley. This was Desmond's last ballet production in his career and was remarkable for its lavishness and detail. He was a joy to work with and an important figure in the history of American Ballet Theatre.

Commissioning *Othello* and *Snow Maiden* was an attempt to add to the company's repertory of full-length story ballets, as were company premieres of *The Merry Widow* and *Cinderella*.

Our major success with staging the company premiere of a full-length ballet was the addition of *Le Corsaire*, a relative rarity that was known primarily for its pas de deux, especially as danced by Rudolf Nureyev. The Boston Ballet had staged a full-length *Corsaire*, produced by its artistic director, Anne Marie Holmes. Kevin had seen the production and thought it would be good for us.

The ballet has four major male leads and two central female roles. It would be perfect for the current group of ABT principal dancers. When Anne Marie came to teach the ballet it was clear that changes had to be made, however. The story line was confusing and needed cleaning up. Kevin worked tirelessly to make the changes required. In his typical modest way, he claimed no credit whatsoever.

But when the ballet debuted in 1998, it was a mammoth hit. The male roles, particularly, gave Ethan Stiefel, Angel Corella, José Carreno, and Vladimir Malakhov a chance to shine. The physical production, originally from the Kirov, was a bit creaky, but the dancing was sublime and the story was fun. It was not high art, but it was a delightful and useful addition to the repertoire.

As pleased as I am to have been part of the production of these wonderful ballets, I know that the future of dance depends upon finding ways to create ballets without the high budgets required by performances on large stages. When the great twentieth-century choreographers were creating their masterpieces, they had the luxury to create five or more new works each year. Rehearsal costs were minimal, unions were nonexistent, and costume and set costs were also low. A work could be created and discarded without a thought.

Now new works are incredibly expensive. Rehearsal costs can be many hundreds of thousands of dollars for a major work with many dancers. Sets can be huge and one can easily spend up to three thousand dollars per costume! When one spends hundreds of thousands of dollars on a work, it had better be good. This puts pressure on choreographers, inhibits risk taking, and vastly reduces the number of works any one choreographer can create in a year or a career. No wonder we don't have Balanchines or Grahams emerging these days.

EDUCATION AND TRAINING

One way to reduce the cost of creating new works is to use younger, less experienced dancers to develop the work. It can then be transferred to more experienced dancers at a substantially lower cost. It is the creation process that is so slow and expensive in dance making. Hours can be spent on a few minutes of movement. One comes to regard highly those choreographers, like Lar or Twyla, who are truly prepared when they enter the studio.

This was but one of the reasons to re-establish a second company at ABT. Gage Bush Englund, a former ABT dancer, had created with her late husband, Robert, a junior ABT company in the 1970s. At one point, they took the company to the Joffrey, where it flourished for a time. After the problems of the Joffrey forced a move to Chicago, the junior company was without a home.

Gage suggested it should return to ABT. She generously agreed to provide most of the funding since we were not in position to bear this expense. After much negotiation, we agreed upon the name ABT Studio Company and, in 1996, the company was re-formed.

The Studio Company had several goals. It provided a training ground for young ballet dancers not ready to join the first company, giving them training and stage experience. Many graduates of the program have already joined the main company.

It also provided a place where young choreographers could work. John Selya and Robert Hill, ABT dancers with an interest in choreography, both created works for the Studio Company.

The Studio Company also played a pivotal role in our educational work. It was far simpler and less expensive to send these young dancers into the public schools. And it worked better, too, since these dancers were closer in age to the students they were addressing than the dancers in the main company.

The Studio Company was an ideal place for young dancers to begin their professional careers, although it was not enough. We wanted an opportunity to work with scholarship students while they were still quite young without taking them from their families for full-time study. We also wanted an opportunity to meet and work with a larger number of talented young dancers. From this desire sprang the ABT Summer

Intensive Program. This was, initially, a six-week training program held in our studios in New York. An audition tour identified those young dancers throughout the United States who would benefit from our coaching. The program paid for itself since tuition was not inexpensive. Scholarships were offered to the most promising dancers. The program was initiated in the summer of 1996 and grew to include camps in Alabama and Detroit during my tenure.

The summer programs were challenging to administer and placed new burdens on ABT, but they also introduced us to many young dancers, gave us a chance to work with our scholarship students, and became a feeder for the Studio Company. They also gave us a chance to work with ABT graduates, from Christine Spizzo to Bonnie Mathis to Cynthia Gregory to Kirk Petersen. It was a pleasure to have these artists back at ABT and to have our studios filled with young people.

In addition to training young dancers, I wanted to use the resources of ABT to introduce more children to dance. Arts organizations must address seriously the lack of arts education in the public schools. For a time, we were encouraged to measure the success of these programs by the number of children reached. A program that exposed five thousand children was deemed better than one that reached one thousand. I have long disputed this view. For me, exposing children to the arts is not enough. A one-off student lecture demonstration has minimal impact (although it is true that a student performance by the Ballet Russe de Monte Carlo first inspired Alvin Ailey to begin dancing). We must create a habit of going to the arts. We must develop programs that allow children to interact with the arts over time and that ideally involve parents as well.

It was this philosophy that led me to develop Make a Ballet, one of the most important programs I have developed in my career. Make a Ballet is simple to describe: one takes a group of children and teaches them to create a ballet performance, from developing the choreography to designing the sets and costumes to doing the fund-raising to devising the marketing strategy.

The idea behind the program was also simple. Too often we expose children to an art form by asking them to participate in creating that kind of art. If they cannot do it well, we simply assume that art form is not for that child and we move on. For instance, we teach a group of children to dance. Those who cannot dance are told explicitly or implicitly that "dance is not for them" and are encouraged to play an instrument or draw or sing. I find this a huge waste of opportunity.

I, for one, cannot dance a step. While I took ballet classes in Kansas City (with Claudette at my side at the barre), I could not dance. And yet, I have had a rewarding career in dance. If my involvement with ballet had been dependent simply upon my performing talent, I would have been so much the poorer. I believe the same applies to children. We must allow children to "enter" the arts through whichever related discipline is interesting to them.

Make a Ballet teaches some children to dance. But it teaches others to design sets or costumes, others to do budgets and marketing plans. Each child has an in-depth experience with the art form and is more likely to care about it than if he or she simply visited one student performance.

With this general concept in mind, I approached administrators with the Department of Education of the City of New York to discuss where we might develop this idea further. The response was unanimous: go to the Frederick Douglass Academy in Harlem, an innovative public school developed by Dr. Lorraine Monroe. Dr. Monroe encouraged corporations and other organizations to help create programs for the students. There were sophisticated computer labs, annual trips to Japan, visits to Europe, and more. The ninth-grade students ran the cafeteria.

There was also a quid pro quo. The students were required to do well in school. Those falling behind had mandatory tutoring. There was a school uniform. Sneakers were not allowed. When one student turned up for a trip to ABT in sneakers, she was sent home. No questions asked. This strict discipline was foreign to me, and not comfortable, but it worked. A huge percentage of these students went on to college, most on scholarship. Dr. Monroe had turned one of New York's worst schools into one of its best.

I was honored to meet with her and her assistant principal Dorothy Haime. While we had feared that they might be hesitant to participate in a large-scale dance program, Dr. Monroe and Ms. Haime were so excited about the project that they decided to make it part of the base ninth-grade curriculum. Students would spend two periods each week in the Make a Ballet program. After a semester during which all the ninth-graders would take dance, each student would decide to join one of four teams addressing an element of producing a dance performance: dance/choreography, costume and set design and construction, stage management/crewing, administration.

Dr. Monroe was especially interested in training her own teachers, and we devised a team teaching approach to allow her teachers to participate fully in the program. For example, I would teach the administration team to do budgets, marketing, and fund-raising. I was paired with a computer teacher who taught relevant computer skills: word processing, computer design, and spreadsheets.

One early concern, of course, was money. Who would pay for the teachers, the materials, and so forth? Fortunately, the New York State Council on the Arts started a program in 1996 that supported partnerships between schools and arts groups. Make a Ballet was one of the first recipients of an Empire State Partnership Grant. Dorothy Haime and I went to Albany together to receive the grant and celebrate with other recipients.

The implementation of Make a Ballet started with an afternoon session that drew parents and teachers to ABT to discuss the project. Everyone was enthusiastic. It demonstrated how important vision and leadership are to an organization. Dr. Monroe's vision had been so ably communicated to her staff that they were all as open as she was.

We also invited a group of students from Frederick Douglass to ABT to meet with our staff and to discuss how a ballet is developed. These were the students who would start in the program the following school year. I think their enthusiasm was infectious and everyone at ABT staff was excited about Make a Ballet.

The actual implementation was even more gratifying. We each went weekly to Harlem to teach. I taught the administration classes; these sessions were challenging but fun. I would go back to work thoroughly exhausted. Jean Jacques Cesbron, who was running our education program at ABT, did a fabulous job of organizing the entire program and maintaining calm when we encountered unexpected challenges.

In the end, the seventy-five students involved had a remarkable experience. They did budgets, raised money, designed and built costumes and sets, crewed the show, and danced. I particularly enjoyed taking groups of students to visit corporations and soliciting funding for their program. During the course of the school year, the participants were all

invited to ABT performances with their parents. This parental involvement was crucial to the program.

The final performance was moving for both the children and their
families. Many of the parents had never seen their children on stage
before. The non-dancers in the program had a chance to discuss their
participation. I wanted them all to have a chance in the sun, not just the
performers.

Make a Ballet survived well past my tenure. Several of the participants
have gone on to internships and mentoring programs. I am convinced
that all of the participants have a far greater chance of enjoying dance in
their lives than they would have without Make a Ballet.

MARKETING

Taken together, the Studio Company, the summer camps, the new repertory, the exhibition, the new tours, Make a Ballet, and the City Center
season created a completely different impression of ABT by 1998 than
existed in 1995. While previously ABT simply danced at the Met and did
some touring, now it was a much fuller and richer organization. The
new financial position, with its roots in the Peter T. Joseph Challenge
and the Mellon grant, completed the picture of a healthier, more vibrant
organization.

If we were to sustain this new image, however, we needed to re-think
the marketing of the organization as well. Bob Pontarelli had been marketing director at ABT since 1980. He had lived through the heady days
of the Baryshnikov era and had suffered through the lean years. Bob
and I thought alike about what was needed: a full-scale ramp up of our
national marketing efforts with a focus on the new programs at ABT
and, especially, a focus on the new crop of principal dancers, especially
the new male dancers, at ABT.

I have long believed that despite Balanchine's statement that "Dance
is woman," male dancers sell a great many ballet tickets. And ABT had
men. Julio Bocca, José Carreno, Vladimir Malakhov, Angel Corella, and
Maxim Belotserkovsky were all at ABT when I arrived. Shortly thereafter,
Ethan Stiefel joined the company. It was an astonishing group.

Of course the men needed women to partner. If our women were
less remarked upon at ABT it is simply that many had been with the

company for years. They were not news. Susan Jaffe, a dear friend, was ABT's senior ballerina. She had undergone a transformation in recent years, adding depth of characterization to her prodigious technique. Nina Ananiashvili and Alex Ferri were both world-class ballerinas who spent too little time with the company. Julie Kent developed into a first-rate dancing actress; I would place her Juliet against any other.

I was disappointed that my tenure did not coincide with Amanda McKerrow's happiest days. She suffered a series of injuries that prevented her from performing very often during my tenure. It was a joy to see her back in prime form after I left the company. There were so many other wonderful dancers at ABT—it was an honor to support them in their work.

The talent and diversity of our principal dancers gave Bob Pontarelli the ammunition he needed to develop a new and dynamic marketing program for ABT. The central feature was to focus on the new stars of ABT. One example: the radio advertisements we used for our Metropolitan Opera seasons had a background voice reading the names of the principal dancers. It was a not-so-subtle reminder of the renewed star power at ABT. This was controversial. Focusing on some people excludes others. There were hurt feelings, but it was essential to get the public talking about ABT's dancers once again and to get our audience to go several times to the same ballet to enjoy different casts.

We also changed the images we used. We focused on dynamic and dramatic photographs, frequently of men in the air. For my first Met season we used a remarkable picture of Vladimir Malakhov in *Le Corsaire*. I believe these pictures are much more inviting than those of women in arabesque en pointe, pictures used over and over in ballet marketing.

Much of our marketing effort was aimed at our closest competitor for ticket sales and funding, the New York City Ballet. American Ballet Theatre and the New York City Ballet have always had an armed truce. We lend costumes and sets to each other on occasion but there is little formal contact. We perform at the same time, each spring, a few hundred feet from each other.

I was frequently asked why we performed at the same time. ABT had little choice when it could perform at the Met. The only time available is May through July, and the earlier weeks are easier to sell than the later weeks. New York City Ballet's schedule is developed in conjunction with its co-tenant at the New York State Theater, the New York City Opera. They would have more flexibility, it seems, to change their performing dates, but I am sure there are good reasons why this is not feasible or attractive to them.

The competition between the two companies does rear its head every now and then. The most viciously fought battle between the companies was what became known as "banner wars." There are several large poles outside Lincoln Center on which banners can be suspended. Some of the poles allow for a great deal more "banner visibility" than others.

ABT, as a tenant of the Met, was traditionally given one of the central positions. When ABT started selling much better, the New York City Ballet argued that we were not a resident of Lincoln Center (which was true) and that they, not we, deserved the center pole. We were relegated to the pole position farthest down Broadway and invisible to just about everyone.

We went into action and threatened to withhold our rent from the Met if they did not argue on our behalf. They did and arranged a meeting with the leadership of Lincoln Center. Eventually a rotational system was put in place and we were promised that our banner would always fly in one of three prime locations. To my knowledge, this solution has stayed in effect to this day.

This battle seems silly in retrospect, but it was a deeply emotional point at the time and illustrates the fear with which we lived. Selling tickets was a constant struggle. Bob and I would evaluate ticket sales reports daily and agonize over a day that was inferior to the same day the year before. We would evaluate our advertising strategy constantly and make revisions as necessary. We would change the content of our ads, the size of the ads, and their placement. It was a painstaking process, but I remain convinced that the tremendous growth in ticket sales during our Met seasons resulted, in part, from this constant evaluation and change in tactics.

We also became much more aggressive about feature stories that focused on the new programs at ABT. With so many new ventures, it was easier to make the organization sound dynamic and thriving.

As each of our new programs was developed and implemented, ABT became known increasingly as a vital and successful institution. Some of this reputation rubbed off on me and the press began to talk about me more frequently. Sid Smith, a Chicago journalist, called me the

"Turnaround King." This sobriquet was to follow me across the ocean to my days in London. A funnier piece appeared in the *Village Voice*. It was a thoughtful feature that compared running a ballet company to running a sports franchise. It began with the unfortunate sentence "Michael Kaiser is the Dennis Rodman of dance." Dennis Rodman was a basketball player known for his unusual antics and hairstyles. To most readers, including all of my staff and dancers, that was the comparison they thought the author intended. His real intention was subtler. Mr. Rodman was known for rebounding in basketball; the author meant that I was known for helping arts organizations to rebound. The *Washington Post* did a very nice story on Kevin and me and the rebirth of ABT and I was a guest on NPR to discuss turnarounds in the arts.

Of all the coverage we received, however, the most important was a piece by Anna Kisselgoff in the *New York Times* prior to the 1996 Met season. As the dean of American dance critics, Ms. Kisselgoff had opinions that carried a great deal of weight. She wrote very favorably about the progress at ABT, our new artistic and educational ventures, and our renewed fiscal health. It had a tremendous impact on the way we were perceived by our donors and audience. I was immensely proud to have my work recognized in this way.

A second manifestation of the changing perception of ABT was the willingness of PBS to film dance programs about ABT again. It had been a decade since ABT had been on television, a filming of *Romeo and Juliet* with Natalia Makarova and Kevin. This was a famous filming where Kevin forgot to remove his sweat pants for the last act and performed the entire act wearing them. The sweat pants were later auctioned to support the company.

Judy Kinberg and Jac Venza, of PBS's *Dance in America*, discussed with Claudette and me the possibility of filming a gala-type performance that would showcase the remarkable depth of our principal dancers. Filming at the Met is prohibitively expensive; City Center would be much more cost-effective a venue. Kevin devised a program that was entertaining and diverse and showed our dancers to best advantage. Planning took ten months and we helped Judy raise the funds for the program. Peter Joseph and Gerry Grinberg, head of Movado Watch and a tremendously supportive member of the ABT board, helped to defray the program costs.

We invited donors and friends to the two filming sessions. Makarova agreed to be the host; she told the story of her U.S. debut, at City Center, and showed the place where she collapsed after her initial solo in *Giselle*. As charming as she is, her speech had to be cut in so many places that one can get dizzy watching her on the tape.

The dancers were fantastic. Susie and José did *Sleeping Beauty*, Angel and Paloma the *Don Q* pas de deux. Julie Kent and Robert Hill did the pas de deux from James Kudelka's *Cruel World*; Amanda McKerrow and her husband, John Gardner, danced Tudor's *Leaves Are Fading*; and Keith Roberts, Parrish Maynard, and Vladimir Malakhov did Nacho Duato's *Remanso*. A highlight for me was the Balcony Scene from *Romeo and Juliet* with Julio and Alex. The program opened with the corps's entry in the last act of *Sleeping Beauty* and closed with the last movement of Clark Tippet's *Bruch's Violin Concerto* with Ethan Stiefel and Ashley Tuttle.

It was a brilliant program and the dancer interviews that were interspersed throughout displayed the youth and vitality of these charming, talented people.

The success of our new production of *Le Corsaire* gave PBS a second opportunity to film the company. All of the arrangements were made during my tenure, although the filming and broadcast only happened after I left. I was so pleased and honored when I was given a special credit at the end of the *Corsaire* film. Watching from home, one has no idea how much time is devoted to planning these broadcasts. While I did my part, the true lion's share of the work was performed by Claudette. She, as much as anyone, was responsible for the tremendous productivity of the organization in the late 1990s.

FUND-RAISING

While the new repertoire and new marketing and new dancers were having a marked impact on ticket sales on tour and at the Met (our box office revenue increased more than half a million dollars in one year alone), the greatest impact was on fund-raising.

I had hired Lynn Thommen to become director of development at ABT in 1997. Lynn had been so successful at the Jewish Museum, a former consulting client, that the entire museum staff and board were angry with me for poaching her. But she was ready for a new challenge and I was thrilled to get her. (More recently, Lynn left ABT to rejoin the Jewish Museum; turnabout is fair play.) Lynn brought a remarkable professionalism and strategic sense to ABT. Under her direction, the organization began to raise more serious sums, building on all forms of fund-raising from corporations to foundations to individuals.

Amazingly, even our government grants increased. We received one of a handful of Millennium Grants from the National Endowment for the Arts (NEA). These were grants meant to celebrate the wealth of American culture. We applied for a grant that would allow ABT to mount and record a series of the great American ballet masterworks, from Robbins's *Fancy Free* to De Mille's *Fall River Legend*. Over a period of years we restaged and captured for posterity an invaluable archive of works.

The New York State Council on the Arts (NYSCA) was also very supportive. With the great help of the director of its dance program, Beverly d'Anne, ABT was able to apply in a wide range of categories and NYSCA supported new works, our New York season, and our Make a Ballet program.

Although government funding was difficult to attract, one of the easiest ways to raise funds for an arts organization is to stage a gala performance. While there is a great deal of work involved in producing a gala, board members typically find it easier to sell tickets to a well-organized gala than to raise money from other sources. (As I learned at Alvin Ailey, if other kinds of fund-raising programs were as clear, they would be far more successful.) The ABT galas raised more than one million dollars each year, a substantial portion of contributed funds.

As important as galas are, they also are difficult to bring off. My first ABT gala was an event called Dances at Dinner, a fall gala for ABT at a time before the City Center seasons had been inaugurated. The event, conceived by Peter Joseph, was held at the famous Four Seasons restaurant. After drinks in the Grill Room, we went to dinner in the Pool Room. A small stage was built on top of the pool to house a short performance by ABT dancers. This was the highlight of the glamorous evening.

Peter loved the event. He had had his wedding at the Four Seasons and felt at home there. Unfortunately, only a few tables had an unimpeded view of the stage, the costs were very high as a proportion of revenue, and the dancers simply hated dancing on the small stage. Eventually no principal dancer would agree to perform on top of the pool. By that time, however, the opening of the City Center season replaced Dances at Dinner and we happily put away forever that rickety stage over the Four Seasons pool.

The big gala of the year was, of course, the opening of the Metropolitan Opera season. These galas were large, glamorous, and hugely profitable. My first Met gala was incredibly difficult, however. To ensure that the performance was a sellout, Kevin invited Liza Minnelli to perform a tango with Julio Bocca. We also had Natalia Makarova, Cynthia Gregory, and Ann Reinking as hosts. The day of the event first Liza and then Ann cancelled because of ill health. Bob and I were convinced that many ticket purchasers would be furious, demand their money back, and cause a stir.

In the event, no one seemed to care. We had a wonderful performance after a day of hell: reprinting programs, placing posters in the lobby, and so forth. Both Natasha and Cynthia spoke charmingly and meaningfully, the dancers were superb, and the dinner in the tent was festive.

The 1997 gala was special for the appearance of Alicia Alonzo, who spoke so movingly about her experience with George Balanchine when he created *Theme and Variations* for her exactly fifty years before. It was always a pleasure to introduce the glamorous dancers from ABT's illustrious past to our audience. It was exciting for the current dancers as well to meet and talk with these legends. It is one of the most important elements of the dance world that three, four, or even five generations of dancers are typically alive at any one moment since the career is so short.

The 1998 gala was particularly exciting since it featured a visit by Hillary Clinton while she was first lady. Mrs. Clinton was a big fan of ABT's and graciously agreed to be honorary chair of our gala. She arrived early and posed for pictures with various board members, gala chairs, and dancers. She was extraordinarily poised and kind. Apart from the inevitable competition for the right to sit with the first lady, the evening was a huge success.

Galas are typically only profitable if a large number of tickets can be sold easily to those who support the company. American Ballet Theatre had several support groups of generous donors. These different groups gave many people an opportunity to play a role. Those supporters not asked to become members of the board of the organization are able to participate in another volunteer effort. Each effort also gives some volunteers the opportunity to play leadership roles.

At American Ballet Theatre, the most active of our support groups was the Golden Circle Council, composed of those donors who contributed more than five thousand dollars to the organization and wanted to help raise additional funds. The central activity of the Golden Circle Council was staging its own fund-raising event, the Culinary Pas de Deux. This was one of my favorite events. More than twenty of the best chefs in New York were asked to provide one dish for a large cocktail party. The chefs were arranged throughout the party space and patrons would walk from table to table tasting the various dishes. A wine tasting was held coincidentally. To increase the amount of money raised, a silent auction was also featured.

I love silent auctions. Items are arranged on tables and bid sheets are placed in front of each item. Patrons walk around and write their bids on the bid sheet. Each bid must be more than the prior one by a specified amount. At the end of the auction, the highest bidder "wins" the item. Silent auctions make a cocktail-type party more exciting if the auction items are interesting.

Many of the objects were beautiful; others were interesting one-of-a-kind experiences. We auctioned off walk-on roles in ballets (the corpse in the last act of *Romeo and Juliet*, for example, though not exactly a "walk-on" role), opportunities to watch a performance from the wings, costumes worn by great stars of the past, dinners with famous dancers, trips, jewelry, and so on. All of these items were donated to the auction and collected by the gala committee. One special item each year was a scrapbook compiled by Rosalie O'Connor, a member of the ABT corps. Rosalie was becoming an excellent dance photographer and her scrapbooks of photos and personal captions were auctioned for many thousands of dollars.

While these galas all raised substantial sums, there were other meaningful events that were intended to create friends rather than raise funds. The most exciting of these was certainly the visit by Kofi Annan, secretary general of the United Nations, and Mrs. Annan on closing night of the Met season in 1998, my last Met performance with the company.

A pre-performance dinner for board members and dancers gave us a chance to meet this inspiring couple. Before the opening of the performance, the Annans walked backstage and greeted the dancers who were performing *Le Corsaire*. As the lights dimmed, I went before the Met curtain, my first and only time speaking from that great stage, and introduced Mr. Annan.

The secretary general entered and began, "Thank you, Mr. Kaiser, for your kind remarks." My parents, in the audience, could die happy. The secretary general then proceeded to make an impassioned speech for arts support and joked that *Corsaire*, with its tale of harems and slaves, was hardly a politically correct ballet. It was a wonderful speech and a great way to end the season.

ABT had the honor to work with another inspirational figure and a Nobel laureate to boot. Peter Joseph had a strong relationship with Princeton University and was intrigued by a program developed by Toni Morrison, the Nobel Prize–winning novelist. Professor Morrison had developed a fascinating program, the Princeton Atelier, which drew important artists to the campus. These artists, such as Yo-Yo Ma, would work with a group of selected students and help them create a work of art. The structure of the program was left to the individual artist and no press was allowed.

Peter asked me whether there was any way to involve ABT with the Atelier as he was considering a major grant and wanted us to participate. I suggested we send the Studio Company to Princeton for a few weeks and have a choreographer create a work for our dancers and the Princeton students. A series of seminars would be offered as well. In the first year, we staged a series of symposia on dance topics from choreography to design to administration. These discussions were attended by members of the Atelier program and others on the Princeton campus. In our second year we focused on arts administration. By this time I was living in England but returned for a weekend with Princeton students. The Atelier was a wonderful way for practicing artists to inform, influence, and inspire students; it was a joy to participate and to benefit from the guidance and wisdom of Professor Morrison.

Programs like the Atelier called ABT to the attention of even more people and helped us to create new supporters and patrons. But we had to develop ways to turn these new friends into donors. Lynn and I developed ABT Partners, not unlike the Ailey Partners except that the annual "fee" was ten thousand dollars. For this amount one received many benefits. If one were willing to commit to giving for three years running, we would dedicate one performance at the Met to the patron.

These were lovely occasions. The donors and their guests were seated in a center box. The evening's program featured a dedication to the patron. After the show, the patron and guests would go backstage, meet the dancers, and drink champagne. The toe shoes of the ballerina were signed by the star performers, as was the program. These made great souvenirs. It was fun to see these patrons meeting their favorite dancers and enjoying the backstage atmosphere.

The ABT Partners scheme became a substantial money maker. But the search for funding never ended. Our first Mellon grant had been so successful that we asked whether we could apply for another from the foundation's new head of culture, Catherine Wichterman. With a background in symphony orchestra management, Catherine was one of the most enlightened givers.

She and I discussed the needs of the company and of the wider dance world. She expressed an interest in finding ways to expand the number of dance companies supported by the foundation. She was also particularly interested in new works and we had several long discussions about the problems of creating and then disseminating new ballets. Too many works get an initial showing and then fade away. I came up with a new idea: the foundation could support the creation of new works that would then be shared by other companies.

We proposed that the foundation give a three-year grant to ABT that would be used to create one new ballet each season. Three regional ballets companies, Boston Ballet, Houston Ballet, and San Francisco Ballet, would be given smaller grants that would allow them to "purchase" the work from the choreographer. But the sets and costumes and lighting plots would be lent free of charge by ABT. The three regional companies had only to commit to doing one of the three works. ABT was obligated to ensure that each choreographer selected agreed to coach these three companies should they elect to take the work.

It was a new approach to extending the lives of new ballets beyond their conceptions. It was a pleasure to work with Catherine on the grant and especially fun to inform my three colleagues from the three ballet companies that they would be receiving grants from the Mellon Foundation. It made me rather popular. The grant also helped create some important new works. The first, *Without Words* by Nacho Duato, was my favorite of all the repertory works created during my time at ABT.

I believe this grant from the Mellon Foundation is an example of the best of philanthropy. Rather than develop their own program into which ABT had to fit, the Mellon Foundation gave us a chance to recommend a program that would truly benefit the dance community. It was also refreshing to receive a grant that was meant to support the creation of art. I am, obviously, a great proponent of arts education and development of new audiences. Unfortunately, the grants from many foundations and corporations in recent years had been focused so exclusively on funding educational initiatives that it was increasingly difficult for arts organizations to find funding for art creation. One hoped a better balance could be established in the future.

While fund-raising initiatives were at the heart of our fiscal turn-around at ABT, Claudette and I worked to clean up our balance sheet in other ways, as well. It was clear that many of our debts were so old that the debtors probably had forgotten, or had written off, the debts. One large group of creditors were choreographers and designers who were owed money, usually royalties, often for performances from years before. Rhoda Oster, my assistant, began a project to ask these individuals to forgive all or part of the past royalties in an effort to shore up our finances. In many instances these amounts were trivial; in others they were substantial. In the end, Rhoda received forgiveness from enough artists to allow us to reduce our debts by $100,000, a huge sum and a big help.

A second source of financial relief was the building we co-owned and occupied. ABT resided at 890 Broadway, a venerable building named the Lawrence Wien Center after the philanthropist who purchased the building and made it possible for ABT and the Eliot Feld company to reside there. Originally, the Ailey company was meant to reside at 890 as well, but the costs of occupying the building were simply too great for the company to bear. The space in the building not used by ABT and Feld was occupied by a few permanent tenants (notably Barbara Matera, the great costume creator) and by transient renters, principally Broadway producers who used the large studios for rehearsals.

As a result, one never knew whom one would meet in the small elevators. I remember entering the elevator one day and hearing one of the most famous of all voices right behind me. There was Julie Andrews! The major source of revenue for 890 Broadway was a Sony multiplex cinema that was located in the ground floor.

The Wien Center was, initially, a joint venture between ABT and the Feld company. We both believed there was a more efficient way to run the building and spearheaded a restructuring of the building ownership and management. The building was extremely profitable and had built up large reserves. I could not understand why ABT, during its darkest days, had not asked for a portion of these reserves. I still have no idea. The condominiumization took endless hours of work. But with the restructuring we were able to receive many hundreds of thousands of dollars of reserves and reduce substantially the running costs of the building. We were able to replace the Wien Center staff with our own staff and ended up with a more efficient business. The Wien Center continues to be a central asset of both dance companies.

While the organization was getting healthier and healthier artistically and financially, we did suffer two critical losses. In early 1998, Howard Gilman suddenly passed away at his plantation in White Oak, Florida. Howard had been a vital supporter of the company and had been extremely generous to a number of our dancers.

More serious to the organization was the loss of Peter Joseph. In December 1997, Peter was diagnosed with a recurrence of his cancer. Peter called me immediately and we met that night at the New Jersey Performing Arts Center during our opening night of *Cinderella*. (Ironically it was the last night I saw Howard as well.) Peter was, understandably, incredibly depressed and left at intermission. I think he dreaded the treatment more than the disease, because he had been so devastated by the chemotherapy he had endured during his first bout.

Over the next five months, we watched as Peter got sicker and sicker. He never lost his devotion to the company; in fact, he seemed to enjoy my visits to his home and to his hospital bed. They were a diversion from his pain and discomfort. Fortunately Peter was able to convince his doctors to allow him to attend the opening night of the 1998 season and to greet the first lady. This meant a great deal to him and to me. While others were concerned that Mrs. Clinton was happy and comfortable, I was far more concerned for Peter. He stayed for the entire performance and loved every moment. A few weeks later he passed away. ABT had lost its most important supporter. I am convinced that without Peter's involvement, ABT would have ceased to exist.

Kevin spoke at his funeral but we wanted to mark Peter's passing more personally and arranged a memorial service at City Center in November. Many of Peter's friends spoke. The artists he supported spoke of his generosity. Toni Morrison told of Peter's involvement in the Atelier. Both Kevin and I spoke of Peter's historic role at American Ballet Theatre. But most important, dancers from the company performed excerpts from a series of works associated with Peter and the company during his tenure. It was a wonderful chance to celebrate Peter and his life. We all left the event feeling better.

With Peter's passing we had to address his successor as chairman. Peter himself recommended that two senior board members, Tony James and Anne Tatlock, be named chairman and president of the board. The remainder of the board agreed and ABT had strong new leadership.

When I asked Claudette to replace Larry Sterner as general manager, she made me make her a promise. She said she would only take the job if I promised to stay at ABT until the deficit was eliminated. I agreed. By 1998, the entire deficit had been eliminated and a small surplus had been established. The company was thriving, it had new board leadership, and my job seemed done. I started to look for a new challenge.

When I received an offer to go to the Royal Opera House I had to inform the board and staff and dancers. This was very difficult for me. After my very rocky start, I had grown extremely close to everyone at ABT and hated the thought of leaving them.

Bob, Claudette, and Lynn were devastated. We had become a true team and they felt I was deserting them. Anne Tatlock and especially Tony James were angry. They felt I had implicitly promised to stay when they were asked to be new board leaders. The dancers were simply sad, as were the remaining staff. My assistant, Rhoda Oster, cried. It was a hard few weeks.

But the company sent me off in style with a wonderful good-bye party on the last day of our City Center season. Bob and Rhoda and Claudette and Kevin all made speeches. I felt very proud to have been associated with this wonderful group of dancers and staff and to have played a role in the resuscitation of the company.

CASE FOUR

ROYAL OPERA HOUSE

(1998–2000)

Simply told, the story of my becoming executive director of the Royal Opera House goes like this: I heard the job was open through an article in the *New York Times*, I sent a letter to the chairman asking to be considered, and I was asked to a series of interviews after which I was offered the job.

This account, though accurate, leaves out many illuminating details. After I read the *New York Times* story that Mary Allen had resigned as chief executive, I happened to bump into Lady Deborah MacMillan in the ABT lobby. Deborah, the widow of the great British choreographer Sir Kenneth MacMillan, was on the board of American Ballet Theatre. I mentioned that I had heard that Mary was leaving and Deborah said that she thought I would make a good replacement. I had not thought about this job before, but I had read a great deal about the problems of the Royal Opera House.

The renovation and expansion of the Royal Opera House had been in the works for seventeen years. The funding of the reconstruction and the cost of sending two major performing organizations (the Royal Opera and the Royal Ballet) on the road for more than two years during an extended closure period were so enormous that the project was little more than a concept for most of those seventeen years.

When the British government decided to create a lottery whose proceeds were meant to support the capital costs of building or re-building arts facilities, the project became more of a real possibility than a dream. But the government made a tremendous political error. The entire first grant from the new lottery went to the Royal Opera House. The press and public outcry could have been forecast. Why was such an elitist organization receiving so much when others got nothing? The BBC documentary

The House only confirmed the general belief that the Royal Opera House was, at best, incompetent, and, at worst, completely devoted to the needs of the rich.

There was some truth to both conclusions. The Opera House staff had done a wonderful job for years of coping with inadequate funding and difficult physical accommodations and continued to produce some of the best opera and ballet in the world. But the planning for the closure period was atrocious, and the costs were so much higher than projected that the organization faced a true threat of bankruptcy. And while government funding in England was enough to make the public and press believe that the arts should be readily and cheaply available to all, this funding was only one-third of the amount given to major continental opera houses. Ticket prices, therefore, had to be higher and private donors were becoming essential.

This combination of political mistakes, television notoriety, financial problems, issues of class warfare, and a large cast of colorful characters created a situation that was fertile for tremendous press scrutiny.

For a period of five years or so, the large and inquisitive British press made the Royal Opera House a fixture on the front page of every newspaper. And none of the coverage was positive. It was a deluge of negative press that is unparalleled in arts history. Three chief executives left within little more than a year. The Opera House was heading into bankruptcy with an accumulated deficit that was going to climb to almost $30 million.

In addition to crushing staff morale and making the organization little more than a national joke, all of this coverage did nothing to help the Opera House raise the $100 million needed to complete funding for the renovation. Nor did the statements by the chair of the Royal Opera House Trust that all donors should withhold their donations until the government offered a "reasonable" subsidy to the organization.

The Opera House became such fertile territory for the press that several reporters staked out at pubs across from the Opera House to intercept information from staff members and artists who went there for a beer after work. Several staff members developed relationships with members of the press and directed all internal emails to the offices of several major newspapers. So every concept, plan, decision, and departure was covered as the latest tidbit of this national scandal.

The parade of chief executives in and out of office made it virtually impossible to attract an opera impresario of any stature. No one wanted to be interviewed, let alone take this "poisoned chalice." But I was intrigued by Deborah's suggestion. I had built a career turning around troubled arts organization and this was the biggest turnaround job in the arts world.

While I was, of course, flattered, the possibility seemed incredibly remote at the time: I was American, I had never run an opera house, and I was an unknown, in both Great Britain and the "opera world." Deborah suggested I write to Sir Colin Southgate, the new chairman of the Royal Opera House, and express my interest. She said she would call him to recommend me.

I wrote to Sir Colin, who had been chairman for about one month and who also served as chairman of EMI, expressing my interest. Quite honestly, I did not expect a reply. A few weeks later I received a call from Sir Colin's office. Would I have time to have lunch in New York with Lord Eatwell, a member of the Opera House board?

Lord Eatwell and I were to meet in a small Italian restaurant in Lower Manhattan. I expected to meet the older, stiff, upper-crust lord portrayed in costume dramas, maybe not in a powdered wig but not far off either. Instead I encountered a young, handsome, energetic man filled with goodwill. We had a long talk about the organization, especially the Royal Ballet. Lord Eatwell was the chair of the Royal Ballet board, a subcommittee of the Royal Opera House board, and a longtime dance enthusiast. He had chaired two dance organizations in London and was eager to discuss the contemporary ballet scene. He also discussed the current mess at the Opera House.

I was right at home discussing dance and I gave my normal turnaround speech. We got on famously and while I knew that did not mean I would make it to the finals for the job, I felt that I had put on a good show.

Lord Eatwell obviously agreed. To this day he claims credit for finding me. He cannot be blamed for this assessment; had he not enthusiastically recommended me to Sir Colin, I would never have heard again from the Royal Opera House.

A few weeks passed and I received a call from Colin; would I meet him at his corporate apartment above the Museum of Modern Art in Manhattan? Colin was direct and friendly. He started by saying that he thought the Royal Opera House should be managed by an intendant, a mixture of administrator and artistic director favored by European opera houses. Since most intendants are more versed in music than in administration, he thought this person would need a good supporting administrator: would I be interested in that role? I explained that I thought the financial and administrative problems of the Opera House were so critical that someone at the highest level and of the greatest expertise was needed to sort them out. I thought the team approach, with an artistic director paired with an executive director, was a more suitable model. I made it clear, though I knew this was risky, that I was not interested in a sub-ordinate role. If I could not work directly for the board, I would not be interested in going to London.

We had a good productive talk and Colin did not rule out the possibility of changing his mind on the management structure. I knew that he had a major decision to make: if he wanted an intendant, I was out. If he liked my partnership model, I felt I had a very good shot at the job.

But then a deathly silence descended. This was mid-May. I expected to hear something very soon since the organization was in such a mess and had an interim executive from PriceWaterhouseCoopers, without arts management experience, at the helm. But I heard nothing. I wrote a standard letter to Colin thanking him for the interview. Back came a form letter, "We have registered your interest in the Royal Opera House." Meanwhile the ABT season at the Met continued.

June came and went, with Peter Joseph's passing and the end of the ABT Met season. July came and went. August came and still no word from the Opera House, just horror stories emerging in the press. During the last week of August, I received a call from Colin: he had decided he liked my management model and wanted to hire me. He wanted to hire Sarah Billinghurst from the Met to be the artistic director. Would I go to London over Labor Day weekend and meet the full board for a pro forma final interview? We would announce my hiring that week and I would start as soon as possible.

To use a useful British expression, I was gob-smacked. I had not had but twenty minutes with Colin and a lunch with Lord Eatwell. I had not heard from the Opera House in three months. Now I was being offered the job. But I was not complaining.

I went to London on a cloud. Here was my opportunity to enter the opera world, and to manage the great Royal Ballet as well. Here was my opportunity to work in a huge, world-class organization that I had first visited twenty years ago on a holiday in London. And here was an opportunity to use my turnaround skills in the most visible and most problem-plagued situation in the world of the arts.

My first meeting in London was with Pelham Allen, the PriceWaterhouseCoopers consultant who was running the Opera House on an interim basis. Pelham was anxious to turn the reins over to someone else; the problems facing the Opera House, both externally and internally, were mammoth and exhausting. He was as gracious as he could be and began sharing with me the details of the current situation at the Opera House. The organization was in a serious financial crisis and had to downsize. A huge renovation and expansion were under way, but the funds needed to complete the project had not yet been committed. There was a big fight brewing between three of the most generous donors to the new building and the government. The donors said that if the government did not increase annual funding, they would not make good on their pledges to the project and the construction would cease, leaving a huge hole in the ground of Covent Garden.

But the mood of the country was not to raise subsidies, certainly not for the beleaguered Royal Opera House. The vast majority of the population believed the Opera House was an ineptly managed club for the elite and that government subsidy was not justified. The press was calling for the end of the Royal Opera House as a producing entity and many suggested turning the Opera House into a receiving house for other arts groups. It was a mess, and, naturally, hugely enticing to me.

After briefing me on this list of challenges, Pelham took me to see Colin in his office at EMI. Colin was welcoming and enthusiastic; he was convinced that we could successfully address each of the central problems facing the Opera House. He briefed me about the members of the board I would be meeting with that afternoon but clearly believed that this was all for show; the job was mine if I wanted it.

I reiterated my great interest in going to work in London but wanted reassurance that the management structure he planned to implement was the one I had proposed. After my sobering discussion with Pelham, I was convinced, more than ever, that I would require great flexibility and authority to solve the problems of the Royal Opera House. Colin assured me that we were in total agreement, as was Sarah Billinghurst, who would be my partner as artistic director. Pelham was not so certain. He believed Sarah, who was in New York at that moment, was expecting to be my boss. I insisted that Colin contact her and get her agreement before we proceeded any further. Colin tried to reach her in New York but she was unavailable. He arranged to speak with her after our board meeting.

My first meeting with the board of the Royal Opera House was not the formal experience I had anticipated. Including Colin and Lord Eatwell, there were seven members of the board at that time. Vivien Duffield, the deputy chair of the board, was also the chairman of the Royal Opera House Trust, the central fund-raising arm of the institution. (British institutions typically have separate organizations that do the fund-raising. It is not clear to me why this separation is considered desirable; as I was to learn all too well, it can lead to huge disruptions.) Vivien was strong, direct, and rich. She was one of the Opera House's most generous and passionate patrons, and also one of the most challenging people I have ever met. At this initial meeting, she was courteous, but outspoken. The other board members were less vocal. After I left the meeting Vivien said that no one in England could do what I did and she endorsed my candidacy.

It was a relatively easy, informal meeting, and I felt I had answered each question as well as I could. I was sent from the room and a few moments later Colin officially offered me the job. I was the new executive director of the Royal Opera House. I was thrilled.

I had less than a few hours to celebrate. While I eagerly anticipated moving to London and working with Sarah to restore the good fortune of the Royal Opera House, I was soon called down to earth. In fact, Sarah was shocked by Colin's call. She believed that he had promised her the top job. She was not willing to share authority with me or with anyone. She sent a very direct fax to Colin withdrawing from consideration. We were left without the strong artistic leadership we had anticipated.

While I was disappointed about Sarah's decision, Colin was more sanguine and was confident that we could take our time to look for artistic leadership. There were more pressing concerns. Colin and Pelham had devised a plan they hoped would satisfy the major donors to the building project, the government, and the fiscal requirements of the Opera House. Simply put, the donors would continue to make their payments to the capital campaign if the government would increase its annual subsidy substantially and if the Opera House would reduce the size of the staff considerably and win serious concessions from the three major unions. These concessions involved canceling virtually all of the performances scheduled for the remainder of the closure period, accepting new work rules, and shortening each performance season for the foreseeable future. It was all easier said than done.

The first step was to announce to the unions that the Opera House would close permanently if new contracts were not agreed upon within a six-week period. This announcement was to be made the day after my visit to London. If the unions were willing to renegotiate their contracts, the donors and government would need to agree on the new size of the government subsidy. If any one of the three sides to this tripartite agreement failed to come to terms, the entire agreement would fail and the Opera House faced the serious threat of closure. I might have the shortest tenure in the history of arts management and lose my job before I actually started!

Colin and I agreed that my appointment would be announced after the union meetings and that I would start work two months later on November 12. (I selected this date so I could complete the ABT City Center season.) I would return in October for a one-week visit to find a place to live and to meet senior staff.

Before leaving, John Seekings, the director of operations and the staff leader of the construction project, gave me a tour of the building site. He was proud of the design and enthusiastic about the capabilities of the new building. All I saw was a mass of concrete; it did not seem possible that the building would be completed in little more than a year.

After I returned to New York, the Opera House announced the restructuring plan. Not surprisingly, the staff, artists, and press went wild. There were accusations flying in every direction. The following week, my appointment was announced. The *Times of London* had learned that Sarah Billinghurst had been a candidate for the artistic director job and the lead story in the *Times* was "Opera House Gets Half of Dream Team." I was pleased that I was considered part of a "Dream Team" but surprised that the press knew so much about the discussions with Sarah.

It was the first important bit of education I had about the British press: they learn everything.

Richard Morrison, then the culture editor for the *Times of London*, was sent to New York to do an exclusive interview with me. He could not have been more courteous or written a nicer article. He was later to become one of the Opera House's harshest critics, but for a few days at least, he was on our side. Judy Grahme, our head of marketing and press, felt that the Morrison piece should be an exclusive. She allowed one other British journalist, Norman Lebrecht, to "ask me three questions on the phone." I was to get to know Norman well and, in retrospect, was not surprised that his "three questions" took forty-five minutes to ask and answer.

All in all, the press response to my appointment was positive. Someone uncovered the *Chicago Tribune* article that dubbed me the "Turn-around King," and the title was used liberally. Norman was pleasant, though he said his calls to "the music establishment in New York" suggested that no one knew who I was. The nastiest comments were from the *Financial Times*. The journalist wrote that my appointment was "the worst disaster to hit Covent Garden since the bombs of World War II." The writer believed that the shortened seasons the board was proposing for the first few years after re-opening were somehow inspired by my being American.

I read this bleak assessment on my trip to London during October. I was ostensibly there to find a flat to rent. Pelham had so loaded my schedule with meetings with staff, government officials, artists, and board members, however, that I had less than one hour to accomplish this task. As I disembarked at Heathrow, I was greeted by headlines that Bernard Haitink, the venerable music director of the Royal Opera House, was considering resigning given the terrible financial situation, the severe cutbacks to performances during the remainder of the closure period, and the shorter seasons that were proposed for the re-opening years. In addition, Bernard believed that he had not been informed of the restructuring plan in a collegial manner; he had simply received a short fax from Colin. The press had a field day. Bernard was immediately deified and Colin was cast as the villain.

Unfortunately Colin made an easy target. When he held a press conference shortly after his appointment as chairman earlier that year, he was goaded by the press to make an unfortunate statement that he would not want to sit next to someone at the opera who wore "a dirty t-shirt and smelly trainers [sneakers]." This injudicious statement, of course, was used to suggest that he was an elitist snob. Throughout my tenure, Colin was cast as the bad guy, against Bernard, against Vivien, against me. He was a very committed and loyal chairman and deserved better.

During my trip in October, I was fully briefed by Pelham about the progress with the union contracts, the donors, and government grants. It appeared that the union contracts would be settled, although there was a strong sentiment among the dancers of the Royal Ballet that a shortened season would not be feasible. While virtually every American company danced, and was paid, for forty or fewer weeks each year, the European belief is that a company must work fifty-two weeks (apart from holidays) to maintain the quality of performances. The dancers were threatening to secede and to start their own ballet company. I was certain there was a way out of this controversy.

A bigger challenge, however, would be to induce the government to increase the annual subsidy enough to satisfy the major donors to the redevelopment campaign. I was not at all certain this would happen. If not, there was the distinct possibility that the Opera House would go bankrupt.

I returned to New York and prepared for my big move. During my last month in New York, Judy Grahme resigned. This became front-page news in London. She had felt unsupported by the board. After spending so much time with her on the announcement of my appointment, I felt a bit betrayed.

On November 4, the moving men emptied my New York apartment. At exactly the same time, a big meeting was under way in London; the major donors were sitting down with government ministers to hear their funding plans. As the last piece of my furniture was being taken down in the elevator, the phone rang. It was Pelham. How did the meeting go?, I inquired. Pelham had but two words for me, "Not well." I sat in my empty apartment and wondered whether I should have the moving men take all the furniture back upstairs. I was in the process of shipping everything I owned across the ocean when there was a very real possibility that the Opera House would be closed before my possessions hit British soil.

I decided that I had gone this far and must play my role until the end. I was, after all, the Turnaround King, and I could not escape now. On

November 8 I had my last ABT performance, on November 10 I flew to London, and on November 12 I started my tenure at the Royal Opera House. Paparazzi were at the door of the Opera House offices to document my first day on the job; the *Daily Telegraph* ran a headline, "Chaos Reigns as Kaiser Enters Opera House." It all felt a bit surreal.

While chaos was *not* reigning in our offices, my first day coincided with a march on 10 Downing Street by the staff and artists of the Royal Opera House demanding an increased subsidy. I don't think the march had any impact apart from emptying our offices on my first day at work.

Despite this show of defiance, the staff of the Royal Opera House was always extremely open and welcoming to me. In most troubled organizations, the staff will support your work once it is clear that you offer hope and excitement. I spent most of the first several weeks with my senior staff, but I did make an effort to meet every employee, traveling around London to every workshop and theater where our employees were scattered during the closure period. In my third week, on Thanksgiving, the mailroom staff cooked a turkey for me so I would not feel homesick on this most American of holidays; it was a tremendously gracious thing to do.

While the staff was uniformly welcoming, the press was not. There were daily calls for the closure of the Opera House and great skepticism that the new Opera House would be completed on time. I was unfailingly optimistic in public. And, as always, I restricted the number of people who were allowed to talk with the press. This seemed to disconcert the press, who were accustomed to dealing with more sober British arts managers and who had had access to every staff member, board member, and artist until I arrived.

The press attention spurred numerous members of the public to write to me suggesting how the problems at the Opera House should be remedied. The most chilling letter I received that first week was a simple postcard: "Please let the patient die. Its death screams are disturbing the peace of Gloucestershire."

Disturbing my peace were the unfinished negotiations with the unions, the donors, and the government. Pelham was fantastic; he worked tirelessly on the government/donor detente. Mike Morris, our head of human resources, worked on the union negotiations. I tried to develop a plan for the future, not certain there would be one. The first thing I needed to do was to persuade Bernard to retract his threatened resignation. We met in his office. He was sweet and supportive and exhausted by the traumas of the past year. I explained that I was there to support the artists, to find new resources, to put an end to the constant high drama. Bernard was impressed and agreed to stay. He asked me to restore the performances of Benjamin Britten's *Paul Bunyan* scheduled for the following spring. I promised to try.

The first two weekends of my time in Great Britain were spent not in London but in Belfast, Northern Ireland. The Royal Ballet was on tour for two weeks, taking the company to Belfast for the first time ever. It was great fun to meet the dancers and to see performances of MacMillan's *Manon* and an all-Ashton program. Less fun was dealing with the decision of five male dancers to leave the Royal to create a new company. Given the weakened state of the organization and the delicate union negotiations, these defections were very untimely. Naturally, the press predicted the imminent demise of the entire Royal Ballet. I was convinced that these defecting dancers could be replaced by better performers. But it was impossible to suggest this publicly during this tense period.

Fortunately, after the tour, I was able to sit down with the Royal Ballet dancers and their union representatives and work out a new contract. We did not reduce the number of weeks of work, but we did radically simplify the work rules.

While putting out these fires, I was working on a longer-term plan for our turnaround. The plan focused on creating programming for the new building, enhancing the marketing program, developing educational programming, reducing the size of the administrative staff, and increasing private fund-raising. The key to increasing fund-raising was to begin to create a new image for the Opera House. We had to convince the government and the public that we were well managed, poised to present great programming in the new facility, and able to meet the needs of a diverse nation.

As I was working on this plan with the senior staff, there was a breakthrough in the donor/government negotiations. The government was willing to increase our subsidy to levels that were acceptable to the donors. The immediate threat of closure was removed, and we could get back to raising money, to completing the new building, to restructuring the staff, and to mounting those few closure performances still on the schedule.

Although our focus was squarely on completing the new building and preparing for the re-opening, there were still performances by both the Royal Opera and the Royal Ballet at theaters throughout London. The Royal Opera performed new productions of Smetana's *Bartered Bride* and Rimsky-Korsakov's *The Golden Cockerel* at the new Sadler's Wells theater. Neither production was especially distinguished, and both proved difficult to sell. The Royal Ballet performed *Cinderella, La Fille mal Gardée,* and *Romeo and Juliet* at Royal Festival Hall. These performances sold well and were critically well received. While I attended most performances, it was difficult to get to know the dancers and the musicians when they were performing miles apart.

I would spend all day at the office and every evening in the theater, not an uncommon pattern in the arts but a challenging schedule to maintain in the pressurized environment in which we were working. Every day, it seemed, there were stories in the press attacking the Opera House, our board, and our artistic contribution. We had to change people's minds and we did not have a lot of time to do so. But with so few performances available to the public, there was little we could point to with pride.

It was obvious that the remaining year of closure was not going to be filled with artistic highlights. While a few operas and ballets were scheduled, most had been cancelled. I had managed to salvage the *Paul Bunyan* that Bernard wanted reinstated, but that was the only opera performed in 1998 before the re-opening in December. The Royal Ballet had more performances planned (and tours to China and Japan) but nothing that would generate substantial press attention. We simply had to turn attention to the re-opening. This meant detailing the very exciting programming we could offer in the new house and reminding people that re-opening was going to happen, on time, on December 1, 1999, less than a year away.

The programming challenge was not difficult to meet. The new Opera House would have three performing spaces: the main auditorium, the Studio Theatre, and the Studio Upstairs. The re-opening season was scheduled to include an opening gala, a new production of *Falstaff* starring Bryn Terfel, Ligeti's *Le Grand Macabre,* Harrison Birtwhistle's *Gawain,* Martinu's *The Greek Passion,* Renée Fleming in *Rosenkavalier,*

Roberto Alagna and Angela Gheorgiu in *Romeo et Juliette,* and an all-star *Meistersinger,* not to mention a full ballet program.

While the number of new opera productions was limited in our first season, the Royal Ballet had a more adventuresome season planned. The initial set of performances would include new works by two British choreographers, Siobhan Davies and Ashley Page, and a series of smaller works by noted choreographers. I had suggested this element to Sir Anthony Dowell after a third British choreographer had dropped out of the opening program. These performances gave our audiences the opportunity to enjoy the work of Peter Martins, John Neumeier, Twyla Tharp, Maurice Béjart, Nacho Duato, and several others. The ballet season also included a remounting of Dame Ninette de Valois's production of *Coppelia,* an all-Ashton program, and a Diaghilev program that included four works commissioned by that great impresario.

The first year in the new Opera House also included a two-week season by the Royal Ballet in the Studio Theatre, intended to be a festival of works by emerging choreographers. The Studio Theatre was a new 450-seat theater that was first designed to house the rehearsals of the orchestra of the Royal Opera House. As the planning for the building was completed, it was decided to build a proper small theater to house performances of opera and ballet on an intimate scale. When the board was announcing the cutbacks to the initial seasons and the need to reduce staff size, they also announced that the Studio Theatre would not house any programming for the first few seasons after opening.

Although this seems ridiculous in retrospect, it seemed reasonable at the time. It would have taken millions of pounds to produce opera and ballet in the Studio Theatre, and we simply did not have the money. I believed that using the Studio Theatre would be a clear signal that we were committed to new programming and to arts education. I had to find a way to use the theater without spending a great deal of money. My proposal included introducing some low-cost programming, such as weekly free concerts on Monday lunch hours; programming a series of educational activities; and offering other arts organizations the use of the Studio Theatre, at no rent, if they bore the cost of production. This allowed us to offer hundreds of performances and serve the needs of the arts community, while not increasing our budget.

The Studio Upstairs was a large ballet studio that had bleacher seating and the capacity to be used as a "black box" dance theater. It was an ideal venue for introducing edgier choreography and performance art to the Opera House.

While I was certain that announcing the new season would generate a great deal of interest, there was still a good deal of doubt about our ability to re-open on time. I felt we could combat this skepticism by announcing detailed plans for the re-opening celebrations. This was especially important since the press was ready to pounce if we opened the new house with an "elitist" gala. Vivien, however, felt strongly that the donors to the campaign deserved the first opportunity to see the new building. I was challenged to develop a series of opening celebrations that gave everyone a chance to participate.

I proposed a series of events: a private dinner on stage for the major donors, a children's performance in the Studio Theatre, open days for our patrons at all levels of giving, free performances for the arts community, and the obligatory gala. But we decided to perform the gala twice, once for the donors, a second time for the public. And we persuaded BBC to televise the gala so everyone in the nation could see it. Taken as a package these events gave many constituencies a chance to celebrate. But I wanted one more event to suggest that we did believe this was an institution meant to serve the entire nation. I decided that the very first performance in the new house should be a "hard hat" performance, a free performance for those men and women who had built it.

The announcement of this performance suggested a new outlook at the Royal Opera House. It was announced at the same time as we announced the first season of opera and ballet and the new ticket pricing at the Opera House.

Ticket prices were a major issue. How could the government support an institution that charged so much for its seats? I completely sympathized with this viewpoint, though I also knew we had to balance our books. The increase in government subsidy announced in December gave us some pricing flexibility, and we lowered prices substantially in most sections of the house.

Ticket availability was also a problem. In the past, our major donors and our Friends of Covent Garden, a group of supporters who each gave fifty-five pounds each year to join, were given an opportunity to purchase tickets before the box office was open to the public. Because we had more than twenty thousand Friends before closure, the tickets to the most sought-after events were sold out before the public had any chance to buy. I felt this was unfair and wrong in light of our government subsidy. I promised that at least 20 percent of the tickets at every price range for every performance would be held for public sale. (For the less popular performances, there was a much higher proportion of seats available to the public; on average, 60 percent of the seats for an entire season were sold through the regular box office channels.) While this was a huge improvement in accessibility, some of the press wrote that the "elitist Opera House" was only allowing the public to buy 20 percent of the seats and that "the rich" were getting the other 80 percent. Our Friends were hardly a group of rich toffs; they represented the entire spectrum of society. They, too, were angry with my new plan since they now had an opportunity to purchase fewer seats. I was the villain to everyone, but I still think the decision was correct.

While the ticket pricing scheme and the accessibility plan were widely covered in the press, I was disappointed that so little attention was paid to the programming announcement. Rodney Milnes, writing in the *London Times*, suggested that the programming was a bit more adventurous than he had feared it might be. The ballet press seemed more excited than the opera press by the planned season, but there was relatively little comment. After the bashing we regularly took in the press, we considered that a good sign. The public was more effusive and expressed a great deal of interest and excitement in our re-opening plans.

Although it was wonderful to turn a corner with the public, there were still questions about our ability to complete the building on time. We decided to create an event that suggested the building was progressing well and that gave the press a look at the new spaces in the Opera House.

We held a "topping out" ceremony celebrating the completion of the roof in Floral Hall, the architectural centerpiece of the new development, in mid-February, just two weeks after announcing the season. Chris Smith, the secretary of state for culture, media and sport, gave a wonderful speech that lauded what we had accomplished in the past three months. It was the first governmental endorsement of the Opera House in years. Hundreds of journalists, donors, and artists attended the ceremony, which was truly electric. We released computer-generated renderings of the new spaces at the Opera House. Every newspaper printed them, in color, and a very positive feeling was generated.

The only blot on the day was my appearance on *Newsnight*, a daily late-evening program on BBC television. The interviewer ignored the excitement of the day, grilled me mercilessly about the past problems of the Opera House, and played a video of many people criticizing the house, including two members of the chorus who said they wished the Opera House would be torn down. It made for a depressing end to a great day.

But despite *Newsnight*, the tide had turned and people were developing more confidence in the Opera House. Norman Lebrecht, arts columnist for the *Daily Telegraph*, wrote a front-page story with the headline "Miracle at the Garden." It outlined the progress we had made and revealed that we were poised to eliminate our entire accumulated deficit.

The entire staff had been working incredibly hard during this period, to complete long-term financial plans, to create programming, to finish the building, and to develop the systems that would operate the building, from catering to ticket sales to security. It was a vast undertaking.

While I spent most of my time working with my staff to accomplish each of these tasks, I also devoted a large amount to meeting influential people in politics, the arts, and the press. Two weeks after arriving in London, and before any of the good feelings were generated by our announcements regarding the re-opening season or the topping out ceremony, I had my first experience with royalty. I was going to meet Her Royal Highness Princess Margaret, president of the Royal Ballet, at a performance at White Lodge, the home of the younger students of the Royal Ballet School.

I was going to travel to White Lodge by taxi after a meeting with Colin in his EMI office. When I left Colin's office, I was stuck in a monumental traffic jam. I realized I would have a better chance of leaving for White Lodge on time if I walked back to my office. I opened the door of the taxi just as a man on a motor scooter sped by and I knocked him perfectly off his bike with the taxi door.

All hell broke loose.

The taxi driver started screaming at me. The driver of the bike, who was, fortunately, unhurt, screamed at me. The people on the curbside who had witnessed the accident screamed at me. After I was certain that the bike rider was unhurt, I began to worry about the press. I could imagine the headline "New Opera Boss Maims Driver" or some other such thing. A policewoman materialized and checked to make sure the rider was unharmed. She told me I was free to go. I was convinced that I would be sent to prison or involved in a protracted lawsuit.

The trip to White Lodge took forever. By the time I arrived, the show had already begun. I had been late to meet the Princess. One is not late to meet royalty. I sat in the back of the White Lodge theater, simply mortified by my tardiness and by the accident. At interval, I was moved beside the Princess, who seemed unamused by my late arrival but was pleasant nonetheless. This was my first time saying the dreaded "Your Royal Highness," which I had practiced over and over. I was certain everyone would laugh as I said these strange words and I did stumble over them, but no one seemed to notice me at all. I was thankful all of the conversation focused on the young dancers and their creations. Princess Margaret had a deep love of ballet, and her comments on the choreography and the dancers were astute and moving.

On the way home from White Lodge I became convinced that I was in deep trouble and would be put away for my carelessness. I spent the weekend in my flat absolutely miserable and questioned whether or not I should fly back to New York. The gloom and fear were palpable and I never fully lost them during my entire stay in England.

I next met Princess Margaret at a much happier occasion. Lord and Lady Sainsbury wanted me to spend some time with the Princess and arranged for a private lunch in their beautiful home. Once again I was deeply impressed by Her Royal Highness's knowledge of ballet and her down to earth talk about the dancers and choreographers of the past. I talked a bit about my hopes for the future of the Royal Ballet and for the successor to Sir Anthony Dowell, who was planning to retire in 2001.

Princess Margaret is the president of the Royal Ballet. I first met the patron of the Royal Opera, His Royal Highness the Prince of Wales, on a tour of our building site. The Prince is a great lover of opera and was distressed by the problems at the Opera House. He was most anxious that matters be sorted.

While this meeting was in hardhats and steel-capped boots, future encounters with His Royal Highness were far more glamorous. I attended a gala for the National Opera Studio at St. James Palace and met

Dame Kiri Te Kanawa. I was also invited to a performance and dinner at Buckingham Palace given by the Royal Philharmonic and the Kirov, with guest artist Plácido Domingo, all led by the great maestro Valery Gergiev. This was the glamorous event one only dreams about.

While she attended the Buckingham Palace event, Vivien had been openly angry with the Prince for hosting the Kirov gala and showing so much public support for Gergiev. She believed as patron of the Royal Opera he owed the national opera company his support as well. In response, the Prince agreed to host a benefit for the Royal Opera at Windsor Castle in the autumn of 1999. The Windsor gala was meant to even the accounts.

Windsor, of course, had been devastated by a fire, and this was an opportunity for our gala participants to see the refurbished castle. We took an advance trip to the castle and were awed by the splendor. It was an ideal place for a major fund-raising event.

The evening began with a cocktail reception for our three hundred guests in the grand reception room, all gold and white with a huge malachite urn that had not been damaged by the fire and, indeed, was too heavy to be moved during the restoration. A concert followed in the ballroom. Bernard conducted the soloists of the Royal Opera House in the *Siegfried Idyll*. (Bernard wanted to back out at the last moment but Vivien convinced him he was essential.) Thomas Hampson, Ian Bostridge, and Marie McLaughlin all sang beautifully and the evening concluded with the *Trout Quintet*. I acted as host and joked after the Wagner that if Wotan had had Vivien on his team, she would have raised the money needed to pay for Valhalla and the entire Ring Cycle would not have happened. Everyone seemed to enjoy the joke, even Vivien.

After the concert I introduced the Prince to all of the performers. It was my first opportunity to meet Camilla Parker-Bowles, who has a keen interest in music. The dinner, in a long and magisterial hall, was glamorous and the evening ended with bagpipers beating the retreat.

All in all, it was a hugely successful event and raised more than £300,000, enough to pay for the refurbishment of the orchestra pit in the new Opera House, the stated purpose for the event.

The Windsor gala did not just raise funds, however. It was a spectacular prelude to our re-opening and convinced our major donors that we were back, for real. The Opera House had nothing to be ashamed of anymore, and we were going to be the source of elegant entertainment in the future.

If this sounds elitist, it is not meant to do so. Any arts organization that relies on a variety of funding sources must satisfy many masters. One has to be open and accessible to the general public but also be available to cater to the needs of those who will help pay for this accessibility. This balance is easier to achieve in the United States, where the benefits accorded to donors are not resented as they typically were in the United Kingdom. The British press tended to make villains of those arts organizations that raised funds and even of those who gave them. This did not make raising funds any easier.

I was particularly criticized for accepting a large pledge from an American donor, Alberto Vilar. Mr. Vilar had offered to contribute ten million pounds to the Opera House to underwrite the cost of refurbishing Floral Hall, the nineteenth-century building beside the Opera House that now serves as its main lobby. Colin suggested to Alberto that he might wish to dedicate the Floral Hall to the Queen Mother, who was in her 100th year. Alberto agreed. At the dedication ceremony, Her Majesty seemed genuinely pleased with the Floral Hall and gave a lovely speech thanking Alberto for his generosity to the British people. It seemed to augur well for the new Opera House.

The Queen Mother may have been the most inspiring visitor during my tenure but was certainly not the only important one. Virtually every major politician came to the Opera House for a performance or a meeting. David Trimble, the leader in Northern Ireland, was a frequent visitor and a true gentleman. I wish the same could be said for Peter Mandelson, a controversial member of Tony Blair's cabinet, who sat down in my office and uttered a simple declamatory sentence, "I hope you don't fuck this up." Much more gracious was Michael Portillo, shadow chancellor and a true opera lover. Even Gerald Kauffman, who had attacked the Opera House mercilessly during the bad years, was supportive. He took a tour of the Opera House with me, was very encouraging, and even promised to let the past controversies drop. Members of Parliament on both sides of the aisle were uniformly kind, and I treasure the mentions of the Opera House on the floor of Parliament that supported our work. While this is not unusual in many nations, it was a rarity in England.

One of the Opera House's most important cheerleaders was Sir Edward Heath, the former prime minister. While the Tory party was not known for its support of the arts, Sir Edward was an exception. Though not in good health, he was a frequent visitor to opera houses throughout the world. He invited me to his home in London for a meeting. He sat behind his small dining room table like a very sweet and kind Buddha. He also invited me to a lovely lunch in his home in Salisbury, where we ate outdoors and had a view of his beautiful garden and the lovely cathedral.

But as exciting and invigorating as these visits were, there was too much work to be done to spend much time entertaining VIPs. Getting ready for the opening meant re-evaluating every system and every element of the operations of the Opera House. We had to redesign a box office booking system, develop catering arrangements, redesign tickets, establish emergency procedures, and so on. It would be impossible to explain the amount of work that had to be accomplished and to over-praise the staff that did the work. The public and the press never fully appreciated how much was accomplished in such a short period under difficult circumstances.

The first big test was opening our new box office on September 27, 1999. We had installed an entirely new computer system that had to accommodate the hundreds of performances in both theaters and the Studio Upstairs as well as backstage tours, lectures, and more. The opportunity for a disaster was great and the press was out in force to see whether one developed. Would the new systems work? Would our guarantee that there would be seats available to the public for every performance be honored?

We had decided to open the box office in the new house, even as construction was being completed in the remainder of the building. This was a risky decision, but I thought it would suggest that we were truly ready to open the new building.

A huge line of people waited patiently for the box office to open. Several had spent the night to assure themselves of tickets. I arrived at five in the morning and walked up and down the line talking with the hopeful ticket buyers, especially five young foreign students who headed the line. So much for our elitist audience! At ten o'clock, Darcey Bussell, prima ballerina of the Royal Ballet, opened the doors and the new Royal

Opera House started selling tickets. The entire process ran amazingly smoothly.

To accommodate the demand we anticipated, we kept our telephone lines open for two and half days without a break. The calls never ceased, even during the middle of the night. It was astonishing how many people wanted to see performances at the Royal Opera House.

Most of the credit for this high level of interest must be given to the artists and the artistic leadership who had created programming that was in such demand. But the marketing and press staff had created an awareness of our opening that was broad and deep. Coverage in magazines and newspapers, on radio and television, and online was immense. It was a huge accomplishment.

Everyone was working with great intensity and much of this work was rewarding and often fun. One of the easier tasks was to select the ice cream we would serve at interval (intermission). Ice cream is a tradition in England; many people cannot conceive of an interval without ice cream. We had to select an ice cream vendor and a blind tasting was organized. Here were a dozen very busy people commenting on the "creaminess," "taste," and "spoonability" of ten ice cream samples. We were unhappily surprised when our favorite turned out to be an American brand; we knew we had to select our second favorite, a British manufacturer.

While each of these activities was under way, a serious black cloud was hovering and becoming increasingly apparent: the very sophisticated new stage equipment was not being installed and tested on schedule.

The first indication that we had a serious problem emerged shortly after we were scheduled to occupy the stage in the beginning of September. The crew was meant to complete technical rehearsals on several existing productions before we re-opened, freeing up time during the first season to mount the numerous new ballet and opera performances that had been scheduled. It was very clear that these technical rehearsals were not proceeding as planned.

It took entire days simply to move one of the sets into place; the crew had little idea how to work the new stage equipment and less idea about how to determine when a problem existed, where it existed, and how it could be fixed. It was incredibly frustrating for the crew; these were men accustomed to getting a show on the stage no matter what the challenge.

They simply stared as the technicians who designed and installed the new systems tried to get the sets into place.

In traditional theaters, sets are built in two ways: some pieces, typically flat "drops," are hung from bars that ascend into the fly tower when not needed. The larger dimensional pieces are rolled onto the stage and locked into place. In more advanced theaters, stage elevators allow some pieces of scenery to move up and down.

The new Opera House was designed to utilize the most advanced technology. The fly system was controlled electronically. The stage elevators were incredibly flexible. Most important, rather than pushing large set pieces onto the stage, the floors backstage at the new Opera House were "moveable." Sets were built on large wooden pallets that were embedded in the floor. When one wanted to move the set pieces, one simply "asked" a computer to lower the floor in front of the pallet and small conveyor belts slid the set piece where it needed to go. It was a marvel when it worked. But it didn't always work.

Exactly what was going wrong was something of a mystery. Some days it was a software problem with this state-of-the-art equipment. Other days it was simply a bad fuse. Or user error. Or electrical problems. Determining the source of the problem could take hours; the remedy time depended on the nature of the problem. But in the beginning, it could take a full day to identify and fix a problem. And we did not have any time to waste.

By the time we reached mid-November, it was clear we were in deep trouble. Not one opera had been completely rehearsed by the singers and the stage crew. To make matters worse, the new production of *Falstaff* was so large and cumbersome that it tested every piece of new equipment. We had no idea whether we could get the show on the stage, or run it as it had been designed. We also had to get the opening gala staged, the new ballet program prepared, and the productions of *Nutcracker* and *Le Grand Macabre* ready as well. And we had about three weeks to do it all.

On a bright Monday in mid-November we had the first performance in the new house, a recital by the Royal Ballet for schoolchildren in the Linbury Studio Theatre. Cherie Blair attended. I did not. As the prime minister's wife, whose pregnancy had been announced the previous day, was opening the new Opera House, I was in my new office trying to figure out which production to cancel. The most "helpful" production to cancel would be *Falstaff* since it was so large and so difficult technically. Without taking the time we would need to prepare this production, we should have been able to get everything else on stage. Bernard, however, announced that if we cancelled *Falstaff*, he would quit. This was *his* new production and he had been waiting for it patiently throughout the closure period. We simply could not afford to lose Bernard and looked for another way out.

The only other production we could cancel was Ligeti's *Le Grand Macabre*. The great director Peter Sellars had been rehearsing our cast and the production was all ready to go. But we simply would not have the rehearsal time onstage if we mounted *Falstaff*. With no option, we cancelled *Le Grand Macabre*. While he rehearsed with the singers, Peter kept abreast of our stage problems. He was not surprised when I told him our bad news. We discussed options including mounting the opera in the Linbury Studio Theatre, but none of them proved practical. After I told him of our decision, he saw my level of upset, hugged me, and told me not to worry. He then went to tell his cast.

The singers, understandably, were none too pleased. They were ready to perform and did not understand why their production was sacrificed. They demanded to see me and I met with them in the rehearsal room. I explained how we could not find enough technical time to put all of our scheduled productions on stage safely. They were angry and unpleasant. It was one of the hardest moments in my professional life.

But there was worse to come. We had to announce the cancellation of *Le Grand Macabre* and a few other single performances to the public and press. We sent out a press release and the earth shook. After months of good news, the press finally had a good juicy story: the Opera House would have to cancel a production before it opened. I did interview after interview. I was pilloried in the press. I received nasty letters and was greeted with pity by everyone I encountered. It was a nightmare.

It is impossible to communicate accurately the problems we were facing, and the impact of lost rehearsal time on future performances. The schedule of an opera house is amazingly complicated. Operas and ballets are rehearsed during the day and different shows are performed in the evening. Rehearsal time on stage is needed to get the lighting and technical changes perfect. Safety is also a major concern; one has to evaluate every bit of each production to make sure that the performers and the crew are safe. While many staging rehearsals can happen in rehearsal rooms, the technical rehearsals must take place on the stage.

The new floor moving equipment was designed to allow sets to roll easily from rehearsal room to stage and then off stage when another opera or ballet was performed in the evening. When it worked, the system was remarkable. When it didn't work, it was a nightmare. Not only were we nervous that we could not get the sets on the stage in time for the evening's performance, we were also nervous that rehearsals would not start on time.

And if they didn't, the producer of the opera or the choreographer of the ballet would come to my office demanding more rehearsal time, something we literally did not have. They then threatened to delay the opening of the production. Given the huge public drubbing we took for the cancellation of *Le Grand Macabre* and the cancellations of several other performances, this was something we wanted to avoid in the worst way.

I lived in fear. Every time the sets had to move, my hair turned grayer. Every morning I would watch to see whether the rehearsal could happen. Every afternoon I worried that we would not get the rehearsal set off the stage and the set for the show on the stage. And during every performance I worried that the stage equipment would not perform as planned.

The fear of technical failure never left me. I was worried from November 1999 until the day I left the opera house more than a year later. Every day. Seven days a week. When I went away on holiday in August, I would read the *London Times* every day online to see whether a disaster was reported.

After the opening, we realized that we were still behind and that we needed to cancel six extra performances to make room for cancelled rehearsals. Once again the press went crazy. One performance we cancelled was a student matinee of *Gawain*. We called each school, explained our problem, and asked whether the students could attend another student performance. Virtually all of the teachers were sympathetic and kind. They had been taking their students to the Opera House for years and wished us well. One teacher, however, decided to launch a personal anti–Opera House offensive and appeared on many radio and television shows and spoke with numerous newspaper reporters. She had a very willing audience. Another teacher had her students write essays on the theme, Why We Hate the Royal Opera House. These were bound in an album and delivered to me. One essay began, "Dear Mr. Kaiser, we wish you were dead." We were all devastated, especially Darryl Jaffray, our director of education, who spent her life trying to introduce the arts to new audiences.

We were very late on one *Falstaff* matinee and we didn't complete one ballet triple bill, when we simply could not get the stage equipment to effect the change into the last ballet. (I was taking a rare night off and was awakened by a distraught Anthony Russell-Roberts, the administrator of the Royal Ballet. Needless to say none of us slept any more that night.) Apart from these major problems, however, the incidents of performance interruptions were limited to individual moments on stage: the tree did not grow on schedule during the opening of *Nutcracker*; the door did not retract during the opening of *Gawain* (why did these things always happen during openings when the press was present?); the floor would not move during a performance of *Tosca*. Compared with the problems suffered by several other new opera houses, our list of catastrophes was quite short.

There were many problems the audience did not see. The act 1 set for one *Rosenkavalier* performance arrived on stage only fifteen minutes before the performance was to begin. One performance of *Bohème* was almost stopped when we could not change from Act 1 to Act 2 for a few scary minutes. The worst experience by far, however, was the opening of *Die Meistersinger* in April. We had had a few weeks of clean performances and the public believed all the technical problems were sorted. We knew better. In a system this complicated, there would always be problems. The trick was improving the diagnostic equipment to find the problem and solve it rapidly. We knew we had a wonderful *Meistersinger* production and superb cast. Bernard was conducting magnificently. It was to be one of the highlights of the opening season.

The performance started and everything was working beautifully— until the second interval, when we could not get the system to work. The second-act set simply would not "fly" and we had no way to move the third act set in. This would not have been a catastrophe; we could have performed the third act on the second-act set. But it was opening night and the press was there and I knew that if we had to announce the problem we would be front-page news, yet again.

I implored the crew to keep trying and they did but to no avail; nothing would budge. We placed a desperate call to the company that installed the system; they were monitoring a West End musical down the street. They rushed over and fiddled with some knobs. But nothing worked. I got ready to go before the curtain and make my apology speech. As the curtain was being paged, the sets started to move. It was a miracle. I collapsed into the arms of Terry Edwards, our chorus master.

A similar problem affected the dress rehearsal for *Billy Budd* in our second season. It turned out that one simple cable had not been properly attached. This seems to have caused most of the flying problems since reopening; it never emerged again after we learned how to connect that blasted cable properly.

This list of problem days is, of course, incomplete. There were at least three times a week when something was wrong. I would watch the stage from the television in my office and from a window onto the stage down the hall. Whenever I saw a huddle of technical experts on the stage I would realize something was wrong and would run down two flights of stairs in a panic. It never seemed to end.

But the fear, the constant concern about movement, the hourly trips to my special window that allowed me to view the stage, took their toll. I was so frightened that the only public performances I saw in full from the audience were the opening gala and the last night of my tenure. At all other performances, I paced backstage. I was there so often the crew renamed stage right the "Kaiserstrasse." The artists seemed to enjoy my presence but they had no idea I was simply too frightened to sit in the house.

Each event is emblazoned on my heart and affected my confidence. To this day, I cannot sit happily in a theater and watch a performance. I am convinced that something is going to go wrong. Some fear is normal in the theater; things do go wrong. But the level of mistrust I have developed for stage equipment is unhealthy and unproductive. It is a lasting scar of my time in England.

This backdrop of fear and sadness affected all of the opening ceremonies at the new Opera House. The dinner for major donors that was meant to take place on the stage was moved to Floral Hall to allow for stage rehearsals that had been lost. It was a celebratory evening and the donors left happy with the new building. A Friends event was held in the Studio Theatre on a November Saturday morning. I had tears in my eyes as I welcomed these supporters to the very first event in the new house. It seemed that we had accomplished so much, and yet we all felt so scared. It just did not seem fair.

After the children's performance at the Studio Theatre, at which I was a no-show, we staged our hardhat performance and a performance for the arts community in the main auditorium. The Royal Ballet dancers, with far too little stage rehearsal owing to the technical problems, were wonderful and supportive. Both performances went smoothly and were well received.

The gala re-opening of the Royal Opera House should have been a remarkable event. We had spent so many months planning this evening, and so many weeks dreading the possibilities, that the evening itself seemed an anticlimax. We were all so tense and battered from the criticism resulting from the technical problems that despite the grandeur of the event, it was not the happy celebration that I had hoped.

But we tried to put our cares aside for one evening and hoped for the best. The evening was complicated. There were so many important people attending that we had to split our forces. The prime minister was meant to arrive before the Royal Family and to go back stage to meet the artists and the crew. We were informed earlier in the week that Tony Blair did not want to participate in the reception line welcoming the Royal Family. One can only suppose that he was concerned about appearing too supportive of the "elitist" Royal Opera House and wanted to separate himself somehow.

In fact, at first he would not even attend the event at all. We put substantial pressure on Downing Street to change that decision. It was depressing to think that the prime minister would hesitate to attend such an important event in the cultural history of the nation and suggested that he agreed with those critics who felt the Opera House was not of the people.

Despite his misgivings, the prime minister and Mrs. Blair appeared twenty minutes before they were due to arrive. These events are timed to the minute; each royal visit requires a document more than twenty pages long filled with step-by-step plans for movements of the royals, family, the staff, and so forth. When the Blairs arrived so early, we had to improvise.

This was my first chance to meet the Queen. When she arrived at the Opera House, the cameras were in place and the crowd was excited. Her Majesty was gracious and kind to all of us. The Duke of Edinburgh was particularly effusive in his praise of the new building.

We took the royal family, including Princess Margaret and the Queen Mother, to Floral Hall where they met the board of the Opera House and the senior staff as well as the architects. The window on the Amphitheatre Bar was filled with Opera House staff; everyone wanted to see the Queen.

From the Floral Hall we moved to the Crush Room to meet the major donors and to line up for our entry into the auditorium. The Blairs were already seated in the front row of the Grand Tier; I was meant to lead the Royal Family into our seats beside them. The doors opened and I entered. The entire Opera House was filled with a glamorous crowd with several former prime ministers, all of our donors and board members, and a large number of celebrities. It staggered me for a moment. Then I caught the eyes of my parents, who were seated in a box very close to the stage. They could not see much of the stage but they could see me with the Queen and the Blairs. (That had not been an accident.)

The crowd rose and the orchestra played "God Save the Queen." It felt like a movie. This could not be Mikey Kaiser from New Rochelle with the Queen of England at the center of attention at the Royal Opera House. But it was.

After speeches by Colin and Vivien, Bernard took the podium and led the orchestra in the opera portion of the evening. After the events, the critics were excessively harsh about the program Bernard had selected. He wanted to do something different from most galas.

Rather than have short excerpts from a number of operas, he wanted to perform a few major pieces. Since he was so busy getting the new production of *Falstaff* prepared, he wanted these gala pieces performed in concert, without staging. And he wanted the orchestra and chorus on the stage to show them off. In the end, it was probably a mistake. Everyone had arrived to see the new theater and they wanted to see the stage machinery in action.

The performances of the Overture to *Oberon*, the first act of *Die Walküre* with Plácido Domingo (affording me my first of opportunities to meet this great artist and friend) and Deborah Polaski, and the final scene from *Fidelio* were satisfactorily, if not brilliantly performed. I had commented months ago that I thought an all-German program was inappropriate but was told this could not be changed. In retrospect, I wish I had persevered but the damage was done.

The interval was remarkable for the group that met in the Crush Room. The Royal Family, the Blairs, Baroness Thatcher, Sir Edward Heath, the great and the good of Great Britain: it was an astonishing crowd.

The second half of the program, the ballet half, was as exciting as the opera portion was dull. Anthony Dowell had created a wonderful collage of important works from the history of the company and all of the technology worked. The opening film montage was warmly received. The dancers, including Angel Corella from ABT, who was a guest artist with the Royal, were all on form. The finale, with the children of the Royal Ballet School participating in the conclusion of *The Firebird*, was hokey and wonderful. The audience was ecstatic. As was I.

We ended the evening with a party for the entire audience. Everyone seemed to stay and celebrate. We had opened the house, everything had worked, the television cameras had shown the celebration to the nation, and, for a few moments, I could not have been more relieved.

But the continuing stage problems did not allow us to relax, even for a moment; nor could we build on the excitement of the opening to change the public's perception of the Royal Opera House.

With the new programming in the Studio Theatre and the Studio Upstairs, the reduction in ticket prices, and the physical openness of the new building, I had hoped to create the image of a far more accessible Opera House. But immediately after opening, there were a series of complaints about many aspects of the new house ranging from sight lines to pricing of certain tickets to the food service to the youth of our ushers. The press recounted many of these complaints and published numerous letters from disgruntled patrons. One remarkable series of letters in the *Times of London* included a series of attacks about our refusal to sell crisps (potato chips) at our bars. The prime time consumer show *Watchdog* did a ten-minute segment about the pricing of about sixty seats on the sides of our orchestra section. It seemed like overkill.

The complaints about these operational problems paled in comparison to the press complaints about the continuing technical problems, which usually implied that the staff of the Opera House was incompetent.

But the notion that the Opera House staff was incompetent predated my tenure and was difficult to overcome. When I arrived at Covent Garden, the press had created the impression that the artists of the Opera House were victims of an incompetent staff. The belief that "the art is wonderful but the administration is a disaster" was a mantra that was shared by many. From the outset, I realized that this was simply incorrect.

It is impossible to acknowledge each of the hundreds of outstanding employees at the Royal Opera House who did so much to rebuild the institution, but it is necessary to remember that there were hundreds of people who worked so hard and so well and who proved the conventional wisdom wrong. They were a deeply loyal and professional group who managed to double the amount of programming with a reduced staff and yet stay within budget. This accomplishment does not speak of an incompetent staff.

The problems of the Royal Opera House lay not with the staff but with the governance structure in which they had to function. I reported to eleven different boards in my role as executive director! While several of these boards were very focused and took little time to service (e.g., Pensions Board, Benevolent Fund Board), others were more difficult. When I arrived there were separate boards devoted to monitoring the activities of the Royal Opera and the Royal Ballet. The members of these boards had the impression that they were meant to comment on the artistic choices of the two producing entities at the Royal Opera House. This was a recipe for disaster and these two boards were eliminated shortly after my arrival.

The chief problem lay in coordinating the activities of the main board of the Opera House and the board of the Trust, our central fund-raising arm. The problems that emerged at the Opera House before my arrival set a tone of conflict between the two entities. The absence of experienced arts managers before my arrival had encouraged board members to become overly involved in the operations of the organization. The lack of a clear job description for the board members added to the problem. And the strong personalities of many of the board members made conflict resolution more difficult to accomplish. I spent so much time negotiating between board members that I had too little time to implement the changes needed.

This had a big impact on the success of our fund-raising activities. While the Royal Opera House ran the most successful fund-raising program in the performing arts in Great Britain, we needed to do better if we were to succeed in building the programming of the Opera House. I remained convinced that the Royal Opera House could increase its fund-raising revenue substantially. But it would take a concerted effort of both boards and a well-supported professional staff to do so. Jane Kaufman, the interim director of fund-raising, who had done a marvelous job managing the capital campaign, struggled daily to build a solid program. Her efforts, and mine, were consistently undermined by a governance structure that simply did not work.

Before I left London, Colin proposed a new structure for the many boards of the Opera House, dramatically simplifying the governance structure. I was a solid supporter of this plan and believed that the future fiscal and artistic health of the institution depended, in good measure, on achieving a better board structure with clear job descriptions for all participants.

One central role of the board, of course, is selecting the leadership of the organization. Both Bernard Haitink and Anthony Dowell had decided upon their retirement dates prior to my arrival so finding new artistic leaders was an issue from the beginning of my tenure.

The search for a new music director was the first to be addressed since conductors tend to work with a very long lead time, just as opera singers do. Bernard was scheduled to retire after the 2001–2002 season so we did not have much time to waste.

Colin was, of course, deeply involved in this process, especially given his role at EMI. Colin and I met with many of the "finalists," usually in his office. We met with Antonio Pappano early in 1999. Tony is young and energetic and a great talent. Colin and I quickly decided that he was the right choice. I spent many weeks talking with Tony, giving him the information he needed to decide whether the Royal Opera House was the right choice for him. With a thriving conducting career and a very successful recording career, this was obviously a huge decision for him. As part of the discussions, Tony asked me to confirm my intentions of staying at the Royal Opera House and asked me to plan on staying until 2004. This was the first time I had to make a commitment to stay in any organization and I didn't know what to say. Colin agreed to increase my compensation marginally if I agreed to stay, and I eventually did. But it was not a pledge I made easily or happily and, unfortunately, not one I honored.

The announcement of Tony's appointment was treated very favorably by the press. While he was certainly not a household name, the music press knew his work and he was a dream interview, charming, sweet, and funny and extremely knowledgeable about music. He was also respectful of all the various constituencies we needed to address. Tony went to work immediately to plan his initial seasons. Some of the happiest times I spent during my tenure were devoted to discussing his opening season. He always treated my ideas with respect and, yet, was clearly the leader in this endeavor.

My greatest sadness about my early departure from the Opera House was that I would not be working with Tony on a day-to-day basis. I am certain that his tenure as music director will be marked by a tremendous growth and excitement and that his appointment will be considered one of the great decisions taken during my tenure at the Royal Opera House.

The hiring of Ross Stretton as artistic director of the Royal Ballet was a far more difficult process. While there are a number of great conductors who could fill the role of music director, there are not a large number of experienced ballet artistic directors. One either chooses from the small group of directors who have led major companies or takes a chance on a ballet dancer or independent choreographer who wishes to make the transition to management.

Most people do not understand the nature of the job of an artistic director of a ballet company. The artistic director is responsible for numerous activities, including hiring dancers, selecting choreography and casting, managing the career development of every dancer, hiring and training staff, and working with outside choreographers and designers. It is a difficult and complex job and I believe that for a large ballet company it requires someone with experience. There are too many examples of important dancers who failed as artistic directors simply because they lacked any managerial training or experience when they were given the reins of a major ballet company.

So while the search committee looked at a variety of candidates, I believed that an experienced artistic director was the most likely winner. But selecting someone with experience was not as easy as it sounds since the world is not littered with artistic directors of major ballet companies.

Very quickly a short list was established and we met with a large number of candidates. The most convincing candidate was Ross Stretton, whom I had known briefly at ABT and who had done a great job of running the Australian Ballet for the past three years. He was more of an unknown quantity to the British press. But he had British training, danced several works by Ashton, worked with Sir Kenneth MacMillan, run a major company, was committed to outreach, had attracted major choreographers to Australia (no mean feat), and had a sense of energy and maturity. It was to be a difficult transition for both Ross and the company. Whether it was that Ross was the first director of the Royal Ballet not to be drawn from within the company, that I left the Opera House before his arrival, or that he made bad decisions, his tenure was very brief and Monica Mason, the remarkable assistant to Anthony Dowell for many years, was named the new artistic director.

We had the opportunity to begin the process of creating new programs and ideas at the Opera House. The Back Garden Project was one of the most interesting and innovative projects we created. Deborah Bull, a principal ballet dancer with the Royal Ballet, and Graham Devlin, originally with the Arts Council of England and then a consultant, approached me with an idea: the Royal Opera House could give free rehearsal time to small dance companies during the month of August when the Royal Ballet was on holiday. Each small company could be given a short season in the Clore Studio Upstairs in September. We would help the dance companies mount the season.

I suggested that we add an arts management training component and teach the companies how to produce the season, not unlike the Make a Ballet program at ABT, but with adults. I volunteered to teach these sessions. I would work with the dance companies to create budgets and plans, develop a marketing program, and implement a fund-raising campaign. The fund-raising element would address one of my board's concerns: they did not want the Opera House to lose money on the Back Garden Project.

Deborah publicized the program and accepted four participants. Deborah had the inspired idea to ask three Royal Ballet dancers to act as administrators for those Back Gardeners who did not have one.

We met every second Wednesday morning at 9 A.M. in my office and discussed the elements of running an arts organization. The classes, while including some theoretical material, were aimed at teaching the skills required to mount the season in September. We discussed missions and goals, budgeting, marketing, and fund-raising. Each administrator had to develop a plan. Each also had to begin to solicit the funds needed to support the projects. Given the small size of the Clore Studio Upstairs, the four projects, with budgets totaling about 100,000 pounds, would only generate 15,000 pounds in ticket sales.

The Back Garden Project gave me a chance to involve myself with talented and dynamic young people at a time when the Opera House was struggling with the stage technology and adverse publicity that was deeply disturbing. I counted on these sessions and relished them as much as did the participants.

In the end, we met the board's requirement: my three administrators had raised all the funds needed for the entire project. I was particularly proud of these three Royal Ballet dancers who worked so hard and, I think, learned so much.

The Back Garden Project received very good press and one journalist wrote that unlike others who have given their notice (I had resigned by the time the Back Garden Project was completed), I was still working and creating. It made me very proud and pleased that my efforts had been noticed, although the true payoffs were the excitement and joy of the participants when they realized they had the knowledge required to build a successful dance organization.

Deborah and I worked on another important venture. A constant theme in my career has been the search for new ways to encourage the creation and dissemination of new works. The second Mellon Foundation grant at ABT was one attempt to increase the life of new works. But the high cost of creating works has reduced substantially the number of new works created in the recent past.

The Linbury Studio Theatre and the Clore Studio Upstairs gave the Royal an opportunity to showcase new works at a fraction of the cost and risk of presenting them in the main auditorium of the Royal Opera House.

In our first season, the Royal Ballet mounted a two-week season of new works in the Linbury. While everyone applauded the concept, the actual implementation was a bit of a disappointment. Bad luck forced the cancellation of two of the new works that had been scheduled to appear, and one of the first works to be presented was rather weak. As a result, the critics did not respond to the season as we had hoped and ticket sales were poor.

I cannot help but think that the problem lay entirely with marketing. It is hard to believe that we could not sell four hundred tickets each night to performances featuring the best dancers of the Royal Ballet, regardless of the repertory. In fact, we had not quite figured out how to sell the Linbury performances for any company. The experience pointed out the hard fact that the main auditorium, with its red and gold elegance, is a major draw for even our most loyal and knowledgeable audiences.

If we are to develop audiences for new works of dance and opera, it is essential to increase the number of people exposed to these art forms. One of the most important accomplishments of my time in London was the establishment of a new relationship with the BBC. There is far too little ballet and opera on television around the world; the costs of filming and broadcasting are simply too high and the audience is far smaller than for other entertainment programs. We developed a four-year deal with the BBC that would yield substantially more coverage on television and radio; to do this we had to get the unions to agree to a one-time annual payment for broadcasting rights that did not change with the amount of work that was broadcast. This new relationship allowed five full productions and a host of specials and short documentaries to be broadcast on television in the first two seasons in the new house, a huge increase from prior seasons.

We were also able to solicit sponsorship to recreate a pre-closure activity: placing a huge screen outside the Opera House for periodic free screenings of live performances. The first of these was the opening of our second season, a performance of *Tosca* with Roberto Alagna and Catherine Malfitano. Thousands of people stood and watched the entire show. I was surprised at the number of people who joined the mass after emerging from Covent Garden pubs and hearing the music. At the end of the performance, the entire cast went outside and were greeted enthusiastically by the crowd. I am convinced a few opera lovers were created that evening.

These attempts to create new programs and new accessibility should continue to bear fruit for seasons to come. But it became apparent to me during the conclusion of the first season that the Opera House needed someone with fresh energy and ideas to lead it to new levels. I was simply exhausted by the efforts to stabilize and re-open the Royal Opera House. Despite my pledge to Tony Pappano, I knew that if I stayed, I would not be the right person to lead the Opera House. I was too affected by the stage problems and too tired to work effectively. And, despite press comments to the contrary, the turnaround was completed. We had paid off the entire deficit of the Opera House, we had paid for the new building, we had established an endowment fund, we had restructured the staff, we had re-opened the house and debugged most of the problems. It was time for a leader who had not suffered through the lean years, someone who could come in fresh and stay for a decade.

I told Colin of my decision to leave early in 2000 so that he would have a long lead time to find my successor. He asked me to speak with Culture Minister Chris Smith, who was not happy with my decision to leave. He was relieved that the Opera House was functioning smoothly and did not want anything to rock the boat. I was flattered by his faith in me but it was not enough to keep me in London. I wanted to go home.

The announcement of my decision to resign was big news. The press was kind to me at the expense of Colin and others. This was unfair. My decision to leave had to do with my own personal needs, not any particular problem with my board, the government, or anyone else. One newspaper reported that I was leaving because I found the Opera House "too elitist." Another reported that I was leaving because there were not enough good arts managers in England. How absurd was all this speculation. I left because I was tired and spent and I wanted to go home.

The paper that commented on my concern about British arts managers was right on one front: I was convinced there was not enough training of arts managers in Great Britain. A few universities in Great Britain offered training to arts managers, but these programs did not meet all of the training needs of the nation. I was convinced that more private funds would be required by virtually all performing arts organizations; this meant we needed a whole cadre of trained, entrepreneurial arts managers.

The need for more arts management training was one of three themes I highlighted in my final round of interviews and speeches. The second was the need for the nation to discuss openly how the arts should be funded. I believed strongly that the need to defend against attacks from the press and the public sapped much-needed energy and time from arts organizations. If it were treated as immoral to raise private funds and to solicit government funding, the arts were threatened and likely to become more elitist, not less, since ticket prices would, undoubtedly, rise.

My final message was that arts managers need to work together to address the funding problem, to meet the management training requirement, and to fulfill audience development goals. British arts managers were encouraged by the press to criticize each other. I found this both depressing and dangerous. We had much more to gain from working together to build funding and audiences; if we openly attacked each other, the public and the government would be less willing to support us.

I gave this speech on radio, to newspapers, and to various groups throughout London. It was invariably well received, but I was not confident that my words would have an impact.

Between the announcement of my resignation and actual departure, a great many happy performances and programs were mounted. Perhaps the highlight was the summer season by the Kirov (Mariinsky) Opera and Ballet. For eight weeks, these great artists delighted the London audience. In the process, I became great friends with Valery Gergiev, the artistic director and music director of the Kirov. He is truly one of the most astonishing arts figures of our age: a hugely gifted conductor who is so passionate about his organization that he sacrifices personal comforts for the benefit of his great company.

The Royal Opera also mounted a great revival of *Billy Budd*, marred only by press complaints about our use of surtitles for an English language opera. They're customarily used in foreign language opera (projected either above the stage or on the back of the seats), but their use in an English language production remains controversial. We had made a promise to the deaf community that we would have surtitles for all productions and honored that commitment. Many in the press found this abhorrent and wrote in exaggerated tones about our "desecration of opera."

Our new production of *Tristan und Isolde* was also hugely criticized, particularly since in this production, the two protagonists did not touch each other. While there were elements of the performance that could

have been improved, I found this interpretation entirely valid and interesting. In too many performances of this great work one sees two
fat singers pretending to hug each other; I hardly need that image to
appreciate this love story.

But our revival of *Tales of Hoffmann* was universally praised, as was most
of the season by the Royal Ballet. I was also gratified that our production
of *The Greek Passion*, in our re-opening season, won the Laurence Olivier
Award for Best Opera Production, and that *Symbiont(s)*, the collaboration
by the Random Dance Company and the Royal Ballet, choreographed by
Wayne McGregor, won the Time Out Award for Best New Dance. As always in the arts, one takes risks; some pay off and others don't. We must
accept failure if we are going to be creative. Unfortunately, too many
members of the press saw doom in any artistic failure. They assumed
that one bad production implied an endless string to come.

As each new production opened and closed, my tenure was marching
toward its conclusion. My last week at the Royal Opera House was a
blur of parties and farewells. I was meant to have dinner with my Back
Gardeners on the Saturday before I left. After dinner they suggested we
go down to the bar for coffee.

When I entered the bar the entire Royal Ballet was gathered for a
surprise good-bye party. I was truly gob-smacked. Virtually the entire
company was there. I was honored and touched at this remarkable
gesture.

On Monday night, the board gave a dinner for me at the National
Gallery. Colin made a nice speech and gave me a beautiful gift, a gold
watch with the royal crest embossed on the top. I was very pleased and
touched. I made my remarks and was as gracious and optimistic as I
could be. I mentioned that the meaningful thing about that gathering
was that everyone in the room had been instrumental in a remarkable
turnaround. And I meant it.

On Wednesday, I moved out of my flat. It was a very quick process
since I was leaving all of my furniture behind. I had the movers pack my
art and dishes and I sorted my clothes. By the afternoon I was ensconced
at the Covent Garden Hotel, appropriately back on Monmouth Street,
where I had started my London adventure two years before.

The next day we had the general rehearsal for our new production of
La Cenerentola. It was a brilliant performance and I was so pleased that

my last productions were so successful; a mixed ballet bill had uniformly superb reviews, as had *Traviata* and *Ondine*. I was leaving on a high.

Thursday night Lord and Lady Sainsbury gave a dinner party for me after a performance by the Royal Ballet. It was a lovely gift; virtually all the principal dancers of the ballet attended.

Friday was the staff party. I took my assistant, Eleanor, for a lunch at the Savoy and the staff gathered in Floral Hall to say good-bye. Deborah Bull read a remarkable letter that she had written to me. I was given several gifts, a model of the new Opera House, a piece of the old curtain, and a book of photographs taken of the entire staff. I was also honored with a permanent plaque placed at the window overlooking the stage where I had spent so many worried hours. The plaque read:

A Window on our World
Michael Kaiser
Executive Director
From 1998 to 2000

In recognition of his outstanding contribution
to the re-opening of the Royal Opera House

I spoke about my affection for the staff and listed what they had achieved. I was truly proud to be cared for by so many people.

Then the Royal Opera chorus sang "You'll Never Walk Alone." It is a song that has always made me cry and this was no exception. I was pretty wasted by the end.

Saturday, my last day at the Royal Opera House, was spent getting ready for the opening of *Cenerentola*. I was given the honor of moving the set into place, the last wagon movement of my tenure. I gave a lunch for the stage crew in the Crush Room. We had been through so much to-gether and I wanted to do something special. Mash, one of the nicest of the crew members, made a brief speech and gave me one of the Nomad controllers that (sometimes) moved the sets. It will always be a reminder of the challenge of Covent Garden and the risks we take in the arts.

That night we opened *Cenerentola*. Eleanor was my escort. It was a huge success and the performance went brilliantly. After the performance we had a cast party. I stayed for only a brief while and left quietly. I tried to say good-bye to my best friends on the staff and crew and started to cry.

I simply did not want to say another string of good-byes and slipped off to the hotel.

The next morning I went to the airport. Deborah Bull was flying to New York as well and we spent the day on the plane. It was a gradual transition from London, her world, to my world in New York.

Years later, the Royal Opera House still feels like a central part of my life, but also a mythical kingdom off in the distance, something like my personal Brigadoon. I know that I will miss it deeply, that the fears I developed there will begin to evaporate over time, and that the lasting impression will be of a huge accomplishment and a special, magical time in my life.

Shortly after my resignation from the Royal Opera House was announced, I was phoned by Jim Wolfensohn, then chairman of the World Bank, asking whether I would be interested in running the John F. Kennedy Center for the Performing Arts in Washington, D.C. I had known Jim casually for some years and had spent a little time with him during my tenure in London. We were united by both a deep interest in the performing arts and, especially, a friendship with Valery Gergiev, the dynamic maestro of the Kirov. To be honest, while I told Jim I would certainly enjoy discussing this position with the appropriate people, my initial thought was that the Kennedy Center job was not right for me. I had often remarked when we took ABT to the Kennedy Center that there was too much staff with too little to do. (I was soon to learn how wrong I was.) I also felt that Lincoln Center, whose own president had announced his resignation within weeks of the same announcement from the president of the Kennedy Center, was a more natural fit for me. I thought of New York as home and I knew then as I do now that Lincoln Center is the most amazing agglomeration of performing arts organizations in the world.

But as I studied both organizations from a distance, I learned that the organization structures of the two centers were radically different. Lincoln Center housed a dozen or so independent arts organizations with separate managements and boards. The Kennedy Center was one organization with many art forms coordinated by its president. I would have far more artistic latitude in Washington than in New York. I could develop programming that crossed art forms far more easily in Washington. And, of course, no one from Lincoln Center was knocking down my door.

I met with Jim Johnson, the successful chairman of the Kennedy Center, over lunch in London. He explained the array of possibilities the Kennedy Center had open to it. He made a persuasive case and he seemed to think I was a logical candidate for the top job. I met with Tom Wheeler, the chair of the search committee, also in London, and then had a series of interviews in Washington and New York. Carter Brown, the late director of the National Gallery and a member of the Kennedy Center board, invited me to his home for lunch with Alma Powell, wife of Colin Powell. I met with Ted Kennedy (and his dog Splash) at his office in Congress. Senator Kennedy has maintained a deep interest in the Center, which honors the memory of his brother. I met with Dennis Hastert, the Speaker of the House. It was all rather heady. The entire search process was remarkably well organized, very different from my experiences at the Kansas City Ballet, Alvin Ailey, ABT, or the Royal Opera House. And it was the first time in my life that an organization came after me for a job—I was used to having to work hard to convince a board to hire me.

Throughout the search process, I was asked to give ideas of the things I would want to accomplish at the Center and of projects that I thought might make a difference. I explained that I wanted to make the Kennedy Center an arts destination, with people traveling to Washington in order to go to the Kennedy Center, not simply buying tickets because they happen to be in Washington anyway. I would work to gain more acclaim for the Center, through high-profile, unique programming supported by an institutional marketing program. I had had an idea some ten years before to do a cycle of Sondheim musicals in repertory to dispel myths about the work of the greatest Broadway composer. The search committee seemed to like this idea.

Coincidentally, I was invited to a dinner with Leonard Slatkin, the music director of the National Symphony Orchestra, a vital constituent of the Kennedy Center. Leonard was in London to assume leadership of the BBC Symphony. Leonard and I hit it off immediately.

After a three-month process, I was formally offered the job of president and quickly accepted. I would start work in January 2001, a month after leaving the Royal Opera House.

My appointment was announced at a press conference held on the stage of the Eisenhower Theater. I had no qualms about meeting the press en masse, but I was scared I would call it "Lincoln" Center rather than Kennedy Center. I didn't. After London, I was prepared for the worst, but the press director for the Kennedy Center, Tiki Davies, had prepared me well. The conference could not have gone better, and I sensed that both Jim Johnson and Tom Wheeler felt I performed well.

That night my appointment was celebrated at a dinner held in Statuary Hall in Congress, or at least that is how it felt. In truth, the event had been planned long before I was engaged as a thank you to major donors and board members, but the timing was most fortuitous. I had an opportunity to meet many of the major players in Washington and at the Kennedy Center, including several of the congressional members of the board: Trent Lott, Dick Gephardt, and Tom Daschle.

In a *Washington Post* story the next day, Ted Kennedy was quoted as saying that if I could make Trent Lott laugh I was going to do well in Washington. A feature story in the *Post* months later was equally encouraging. It was a great departure from the press "welcome" in London. (The British press made this new job seem like a real comedown from the Royal Opera House; what was this Kennedy Center anyway?)

After this star-studded introduction to Washington, I traveled back to London to complete my tenure at the Royal Opera House. Several senior members of the Kennedy Center staff visited in London to discuss plans for major projects including the Sondheim festival, which was becoming a reality very quickly.

Shortly after my appointment was announced I was invited to lunch by Alberto Vilar. He asked how he could help me at the Kennedy Center. I proposed two special projects: one was inviting the Kirov Opera and Ballet to the Kennedy Center each year for ten years; the second was starting an institute to train young arts managers. I believed that presenting the Kirov every year would add luster to the Center's artistic offerings. And adding a substantial arts management component would set us apart from other arts centers in the nation. Alberto agreed to both and offered a ten-year $50 million pledge to the center.

I returned to Washington twice before leaving the Royal Opera House: once to complete budgets for the following year and once to attend the Kennedy Center Honors in early December. The Honors is a unique event: Washington power meets Broadway power meets Hollywood power meets corporate power. The audience is as famous as the honorees and the stars who go to pay tribute to them. That year's honorees—Clint Eastwood, Plácido Domingo, Mikhail Baryshnikov, Chuck Berry, and Angela Lansbury—were the "typical," diverse, extraordinary group. I returned to London for my final week at the Royal Opera House filled with excitement and pride.

I finally moved to Washington to start work on Martin Luther King Day weekend in 2001. There were many challenges ahead: the current forecast for the fiscal year projected a deficit of more than one million dollars, the forthcoming British festival seemed uninteresting and difficult to promote, our AmericArtes Festival of Latin American arts was horribly behind budget, and the executive vice president, Kevin McMahon, announced he was leaving the day I arrived.

I had little time to ponder these challenges. My first week coincided with the inauguration of George W. Bush as president and I was invited to a slew of inaugural receptions. Ann Stock, the vice president of institutional affairs and the former social secretary for the Clintons, took me to every party and introduced me to everyone in Washington. Everyone. Ann seemed to remember every name, every party affiliation, every history. I remembered nothing.

Just after the inauguration we had my first board meeting. I presented my goal for the Center: to turn it into a true arts destination. I wanted to do programming that would excite audience members, donors, and the press on a national level. I wanted to dispel the notion of the Kennedy Center as a regional arts presenter.

I also had three major programs to announce: the next season would include our Sondheim Celebration, the Kirov Opera and Ballet had agreed to perform for the next ten years, and Alberto Vilar was going to contribute fifty million dollars over the same ten-year period to pay for the Kirov visits and for a new arts management institute. The board response was rhapsodic.

On February 14 we announced the Vilar gift to the press. The Center was filled with press and staff. Jim Johnson and I made opening remarks; Alberto spoke at length and answered questions. He was very much on form and the press response was enthusiastic. We were starting the process of convincing the world that we were a true arts leader, the national cultural center that Congress had named us.

Shortly thereafter, Tiki and I met with the entire editorial board of the *Washington Post*. Even Katherine Graham was there. (Mrs. Graham gave one of her famous dinner parties for me on my arrival. Queen Noor, Justice Breyer, and several other Washington notables attended. The following year I was asked to be the music director for Mrs. Graham's funeral, a sad assignment.) I spelled out my plans for the center and included mention of the Plaza Project. The Department of Transportation had developed a concept for a new Plaza in front of the Kennedy Center; the Plaza would link the center to downtown Washington and would offer the opportunity for two new buildings. I had conceived of uses for the two buildings that could be erected on the Plaza: one would house rehearsal space and office space for us and the Washington National Opera, and the second would house our educational programs and a museum for the performing arts. The journalists seemed excited by my ideas and placed a story about my vision for the future, including the Plaza designs, on the front page the following day. Rather quickly, we were becoming the "hot" arts organization in town.

This impression was confirmed when we announced our season to the press in early March. Not only did we have the Kirov Opera and Ballet and the Sondheim Celebration, we also had the Bolshoi Ballet, the Joffrey Ballet, Ballet Nacional de Cuba, Midori, Josh Bell, Pinchas Zukerman, James Galway, Paul Taylor Dance Company, Alvin Ailey, a huge jazz program, and on and on. I had made the decision to announce the entire Kennedy Center and National Symphony Orchestra seasons together. In the past, each art form announced its plans separately. By announcing the entire program together, we showed the richness and diversity of our programming. We complemented our press conference with full-page ads in the *New York Times* and the *Washington Post* announcing the season.

The press went wild. While the Sondheim Celebration was the lead in most stories, we also had substantial coverage for the rest of the season. *USA Today* called our ballet season "the best ballet season ever." I was invited to appear on the *Charlie Rose Show*, *Breakfast with the Arts* on A&E, and numerous other radio and television programs. The public was excited as well. One donor from New York sent us $100,000 saying that he had never been to the Kennedy Center but was excited by our plans. A major New York arts figure wrote that she would deny it if I ever quoted her but that we were doing the programming that should be in New York and that she was tempted to move to Washington.

Another important couple was reading this coverage: Catherine and Wayne Reynolds. Catherine had recently sold her business for a huge sum and had created a philanthropic foundation. The Reynoldses asked to meet with me and I invited them to lunch. They had read the press coverage of the past few weeks and wanted to know how they could help. They were devoted to the arts, to education, and to quality. I suggested that what I needed most was money to do amazing work of the highest quality that we could otherwise not afford. Over the next few months we discussed how a grant could be structured and eventually they offered a grant of one million dollars a year, for ten years, to present one extraordinary set of performances each year. This was a programmer's dream. We announced the grant at Honors weekend of 2001 to huge press and public acclaim.

But developing programming plans is one thing and implementing them is another. Most of the 2001/2002 season fell within the standard activities of the Kennedy Center. Booking foreign dance companies, managing the National Symphony, engaging jazz artists, and so forth, all demand a great deal of knowledge and expertise, but the staff had those to spare. Creating six new productions of Sondheim musicals was another story. By the time we announced the celebration, we had already been working on the festival for almost a year. While I was still with the Royal Opera House, Jim Johnson had suggested I meet with Eric Schaeffer, the artistic director of the Signature Theater in Virginia, who was directing a musical in London. Eric had successfully directed several productions of Sondheim's musicals and had a great relationship with him.

Eric agreed immediately to become the artistic director of the Sondheim Celebration and contacted Steve to see whether he would endorse the concept. Steve was skeptical. He was willing to discuss the project but was not sure how we could do so many productions at the same time.

Eric and I met with Steve on December 20, 2000, three days after I left the Opera House. The meeting with Mr. Sondheim was a dream for me. When I was asked whom I would like to have dinner with, I would always quickly answer, "Stephen Sondheim." Now here he was. In the flesh. In his living room. More amazing, when we met he mentioned that he knew about my work at the Royal Opera House from reading the *Observer*, a British paper.

But I had work to do. He asked why I wanted to do this. I answered that my goal was to dispel myths about his musicals: that they were all similar, that they were cold, that there were no melodies, and that they were difficult to sell. I thought that if we could mimic a museum retrospective, our audience would appreciate the errors in the conventional wisdom. I wanted people to see several shows back to back to appreciate the diversity and richness of his work.

But I had to convince him that we could mount six high-quality productions, in rotating repertory no less, at the same time. I used the opera house production model as a guide; opera houses routinely mount several productions at one time and perform them in repertory. Eric, Max Woodward (the theater producer at the Kennedy Center), and I had thought through many of the production issues; Steve seemed impressed and agreed to the project.

But first we had to pick the six works. We quickly eliminated *Follies*, *Into the Woods*, and *Assassins* (major New York productions were already in the works) and settled on *Sweeney Todd*, *Company*, and *A Little Night Music*. I insisted on *Sunday in the Park* (my favorite), and Steve wanted *Merrily We Roll Along*. I wanted to do *Anyone Can Whistle*, but Steve felt *Whistle* required too many book changes. Eric wanted *Passion*, one of my favorites as well, and there we were. We all appreciated the combination of favorites and less familiar works.

We spent many weeks discussing directors. Eventually we agreed that Eric would direct *Sunday* and *Passion*; Sean Mathias, who had great success with *A Little Night Music* in London, would direct *Company*; Chris Ashley would direct *Sweeney Todd* and *Merrily*; and Mark Brokaw would direct *Night Music*. Of the four, only Eric was primarily known as a director of musicals, but the group seemed young and edgy and appropriate for this daring venture.

The directors and designers (Derek McLain on sets and Howell Binkley on lights) met with Steve and Max and me at a dinner at Steve's house, where we reviewed ground rules, budgets, and schedules. We discussed casting and music directors. Steve said he wanted all the directors to feel free to do their own versions of the shows; they were "licensed" to have their own visions.

We wanted the celebration to be even more comprehensive than six shows. I am convinced that one way to make programming feel more important is to package productions with other types of programming. Steve suggested a Japanese production of *Pacific Overtures* that he admired greatly and we agreed to bring it over. Over time we added a children's version of *Into the Woods* and one-person shows by Barbara Cook and Mandy Patinkin. We started the entire festival with a symposium: Frank Rich interviewing Steve.

Picking the plays and directors was easy; casting them was a lot harder. We had a secret weapon: Tara Rubin. Tara is an astute casting director, whom Max selected to cast all six shows. Her first coup was landing Brian Stokes Mitchell and Christine Baranski for the leads in *Sweeney Todd*. These two major stars and great talents set a tone for the entire festival. Their casting encouraged other great performers to sign on.

Over time other major casting emerged: Lynn Redgrave, John Barrowman, and Alice Ripley in *Company*; Melissa Errico and Raul Esparza in *Sunday*; Michael Hayden, Miriam Shor, Emily Skinner, and Raul in *Merrily*; Michael Cerveris, Judy Kuhn, and Rebecca Luker in *Passion*; and John Dossett, Blair Brown, Doug Sills, and Randy Graf in *Night Music*. It was a remarkable group.

While we were planning the Sondheim project we had other work to do. I had to restructure the senior staff after Kevin McMahon's departure. I asked Claudette Donlon to join the Kennedy Center to take over its administration, including all construction activities. It was great to have her back with me. I engaged David Kitto, who had run the marketing department for Carnegie Hall for seventeen years, to become our vice president of marketing, and I promoted Marie Mattson to vice president of development. I felt I had a stellar top management team.

We mounted the planned British festival including orchestral, ballet, modern dance, chamber music, and theater performances. While it was wonderful to have the Royal Ballet visit me in my new home, the entire festival did not seem to add up to much. Nor did the summer musical in the Opera House: *Kiss Me Kate*. The Broadway version had been spectacular and had won a Tony for Brian Stokes Mitchell. The road version was so stripped down it drowned in our Opera House. It convinced me more than ever that producing our own shows was imperative.

More successful was the National Symphony Orchestra's (NSO's) tour to Oklahoma. Each year, the NSO visits one state that does not typically host many touring performing groups. In 2001, the NSO visited

Oklahoma, and I was able to witness just a few of the 150 master classes, concerts, school lectures, and other performances given by the NSO musicians. A brass quintet even performed at a special session of the Oklahoma State Legislature. The response of the public was overwhelming. In subsequent years we traveled to South Dakota (where Tom Daschle was the narrator for Copland's *Lincoln Portrait*), North Dakota, Nevada, Tennessee, and Kansas.

The National Symphony Orchestra is a key component of the Kennedy Center. Founded in the 1930s, the NSO merged with the Kennedy Center in the late 1980s. The affiliation allowed the NSO to benefit from the cushion of the Kennedy Center's fiscal resources and enabled staff departments to combine to reduce costs. It has sometimes been a painful union. Since the NSO does not have an endowment that matches that of other major symphonies, substantial annual fund-raising is required. Some of the money raised is designated by the donor to be used specifically for NSO programs; roughly an equal amount is received from general Kennedy Center contributions. Over time, some Center staff and board members questioned whether the Kennedy Center should dedicate as much to the NSO as it does; from the beginning of my tenure, it appeared to me to be an important investment since the NSO is the central producing element of the Center.

Just after Labor Day 2001, we opened our Vilar Institute for Arts Management. Twelve young arts administrators from around the nation and the world arrived to begin a one-year program. I was proud of our Education Department for moving so fast and so well to create this program. We had announced the grant on February 14. By early September we had twelve motivated Fellows and an entire curriculum ready to go.

The Fellows took class every morning; Marie Mattson taught fund-raising, David Kitto taught marketing, I taught planning, and so forth. After class the Fellows worked in one of our departments on a high-level project; after three or four months they rotated to another department. The Fellows also attended most Kennedy Center events and all staff meetings. I believe this set of experiences gave each Fellow a strong background in managing arts organizations and engrained in all of them my philosophy of arts management.

While we had thought through each element of the program, nothing could have prepared us or our Fellows for their second day at the

Kennedy Center: September 11, 2001. Early that morning Senator Kennedy did a live interview on the *Today Show* from the Center; we were planning to celebrate that evening a gift from the Kennedy family to establish an internship program for developmentally disabled young people.

We were all in a staff meeting in our rooftop restaurant when we received word of two planes hitting the World Trade Center. Shortly thereafter, we saw the Pentagon go up in smoke. Within minutes we were warned that a fourth plane was on its way to Washington and we needed to evacuate immediately. The staff of the Center left quickly and quietly. Most of the senior staff joined me in my nearby apartment. We cancelled all the day's performances and events immediately. And then we watched in horror along with the rest of the world.

I felt it was important that we reopen on September 12. I consider the work we do important and I believed that audiences needed solace and inspiration at that difficult time. While most people supported the decision (and the full houses suggested it was a good one), others were skeptical. I stood before the musicians of the National Symphony on September 12 and explained my feelings; they were supportive if scared. Some were angry. Over the summer there had been a management change at the NSO; it was hard for them to find trust in their new leadership in this most unsettling environment.

Immediately we set to work to create a performance to honor those who died on September 11 and especially to console the families of the Pentagon victims. The NSO musicians, and all employees, agreed to donate their service to this project. WETA, the local public television station, agreed to telecast the event. Frederica von Stade, Mary Chapin Carpenter, James Galway, and soloists from the Washington National Opera all agreed to participate. And Mrs. Bush and Senator Kennedy agreed to serve as hosts.

On September 24, just thirteen days after the tragedy, a major performance was given and telecast. All the families of the Pentagon victims were invited. It was a tragic time but the staff and musicians of the Kennedy Center and the NSO came through magnificently. Appropriately overshadowed by these events was the end of our fiscal year. We had managed to make up the deficit I inherited and showed a small but proud surplus for the fiscal year.

Gradually, matters returned to normal, although what the new definition of *normal* might be was anyone's guess. Just one month after September 11, a new form of terror came to light: anthrax.

Our Mark Twain Award for lifetime achievement in American humor was to be given to Whoopi Goldberg. An all-star line-up had agreed to perform for our audience and for a television special. But Whoopi got scared by both September 11 and the anthrax attack at the Capitol. It took days of convincing, primarily by Ann Stock, to get our reluctant honoree to attend her own award ceremony. A second anthrax attack occurred in the offices of Tom Daschle the day of the awards. After this attack all mail delivery to federal buildings was stopped for months.

It was extremely difficult to conduct business without mail. Returned tickets were not received. Invitations were not received. Bills were not received. Donations were not received. And since most people and corporations were getting their mail, they did not realize we were not. So we had scores of angry audience members, donors, and creditors. Unfortunately, we had just mailed our Honors invitations before the anthrax scare as well. So we did not receive Honors orders and had to call everyone entitled to tickets. We had a stellar group of honorees once again: Quincy Jones, Van Cliburn, Jack Nicholson, Luciano Pavarotti, and Julie Andrews.

The process of seating everyone at Honors, and at all Honors weekend activities, is death-defying. There are lunches, dinners and performances. No one can sit beside the same person twice unless they ask to do that. The events range in size from 50 at some dinners on Saturday night to 2,200 in the Opera House for the performance itself. Where one sits is perceived as crucial. Those in the front of the orchestra can turn around and see the president and the honorees. These seats and the box seats are considered prime. The competition for these seats is tremendous. The only fair way to distribute them is to offer the first choice of seats to those who contribute the most. Needless to say, there is much jockeying for position, many threats, and numerous calls to board members from people trying to upgrade. I pity my development staff, especially Marie Mattson, who even had her life threatened by one angry donor!

As Honors season ended, we could focus once again on several important projects. First among them was the Plaza Project. While everyone was excited by the concept of the Plaza, receiving funding was a different story. The plan had been to include the Plaza in Highway Trust Fund legislation, but that was at least two years away. I naively asked Senator Kennedy whether we could get authorization through separate legislation. He said there was no reason why not, and we began the process of lobbying for approval of the project.

In February 2002, the Kirov Opera and Ballet made their first of ten visits. Valery Gergiev, my great friend, conducted both *Khovanschina* and *Macbeth*. The critics were not enthralled, but the audiences were. The ballet did not fare much better. The opening, *Sleeping Beauty*, was a faithful recreation of the original production. I thought it would be a good way to introduce the company; I was wrong. The production is long, too long for our audiences. The dancing was good but not great. We all expected more. The next production, *Jewels*, however, delivered what we wanted. It was breathtaking. Only the *New York Times* took exception, though the same critic raved when the Kirov danced the same ballet in New York months later. All in all, it was a bit disappointing that more of a fuss was not made about the visit. But the groundwork for future visits had been laid.

As a sidebar to the Kirov visit, we mounted an exhibition about Rudolf Nureyev, a graduate of the Kirov school, featuring the works of Jamie Wyeth. Jamie and his wife, Phyllis, had a long friendship with Nureyev and Jamie created a number of drawings and paintings. We co-hosted this exhibition, which included the drawings and paintings as well as costumes and videos. It was a beautiful show.

I wanted every presentation to be perfect (and I knew that was unrealistic). But it was clear that the press and the public were focusing on the forthcoming Sondheim Celebration. The day before the box office opened, the *Washington Post* ran a huge story. The next day—pandemonium. We set an all-time Kennedy Center box office record selling more than $600,000 of seats for Sondheim in ten hours. The number of patrons—at the box office and on the phone—seemed infinite. It was a great boost to our confidence.

As Sondheim sales were growing, the NSO was mounting a major project of its own: an extended tour of Europe, a tremendous feat especially with the heightened security requirements surrounding air travel. I was fortunate to join the tour twice: in Dublin and in Paris. This tour was grueling, but, given the quality of the venues, it did a good deal to convince many in the music world that the NSO was on an artistic upswing.

So did our focus on inviting the best guest conductors to the National Symphony Orchestra. I believe that one measure of the quality of an orchestra is the quality of the conductors who are willing to work with it. So we have placed a great deal of emphasis on engaging the best guest conductors. Over the past six years we were able to present Loren Maazel, Kurt Masur, Christoph von Dohnanyi, Valery Gergiev, Kent Nagano, Vladimir Ashkenazy, James Conlon, and, of course, Mstislav Rostropovich. It is a stellar list by any standard.

While the NSO was progressing, many other arts organizations were suffering from the stock market tumble, economic decline, and effects of September 11. Since leaving American Ballet Theatre I had received several calls from its board members about the problems that organization was experiencing. A succession of executive directors had not worked out, and most of the cash that we had accumulated during my tenure was gone. Gerry Grinberg, who had been so supportive during my tenure and was now the chairman of ABT, wanted to discuss a possible merger with the Kennedy Center. It was clear that ABT would benefit from the financial cushion offered by the Center. I also believed that this merger would give the Kennedy Center a true foothold in New York City. And as the national cultural center, we could benefit from an association with a world-class national touring company.

I was happy, therefore, to hold these discussions but I cautioned Gerry that I would only present this merger concept to my board if the ABT board were solidly behind the plan. Gerry had me talk with his executive committee, who could not have been more opposed to the concept. Obviously, their board had a right to stay independent; there are no hostile takeovers in the arts. But I was disappointed that the members of the committee, all of whom served during my tenure, were not more open to a frank discussion.

American Ballet Theatre was not the only arts organization facing challenges. In a speech to the National Press Club I outlined my concerns for the arts environment. I discussed my fear that too many arts organizations were cutting back on programming just at the time they needed to expand. I discussed my concerns about arts management training, about arts education and diversity, and about the implosion of the recording industry. The *Washington Post* asked me to write an op-ed piece based on the speech. I thought the speech and the op-ed article were both correct but not earth-shaking.

Imagine my surprise when Reynold Levy, the new president of Lincoln Center and an old friend, wrote a scathing letter to the *Post* about my ideas. He said I was too negative. He wrote I was a good arts administrator but I should keep my ideas to myself. It was an unusual frontal attack in the arts community of this nation. I could not help feeling that it was motivated by the Kennedy Center's advances in the opinion of the arts community and the coincident problems being publicly faced by Lincoln Center.

The letter was followed up by a major story in the Sunday *New York Times* Arts and Leisure section by Anthony Tomassini, a fine music critic. He agreed with Reynold. It felt as if New Yorkers were protecting their turf and were concerned about the respect we Washingtonians were gaining.

In February 2002 we mounted our International Ballet Festival. Since we were renovating the Opera House, we needed to move some of our ballet series into the Eisenhower Theater. I wanted to do something special there—not just present ballet in a smaller venue. We decided to invite six major companies to the Kennedy Center and ask them to present smaller programs that would work well in the Eisenhower.

The first week included the Royal Danish Ballet in Bournonville excerpts, the Bolshoi Ballet in a potpourri of Russian gala-type pieces, and American Ballet Theatre in *Fancy Free*. Week two included Miami City Ballet in *The Four Temperaments*, the Kirov Ballet in the Shades Scene from *La Bayadere*, and a group of English dancers led by Adam Cooper in a MacMillan piece. (Originally the Royal Ballet was to have been the British representative, but owing to a new production of *Sleeping Beauty* they had to cancel. I felt that having Adam, a former Royal principal, in a MacMillan piece—it was the tenth anniversary of his death—made great sense as a substitute.)

My goal was to show the differences in national styles and the diversity of "classical" ballet. I think we did that and the audiences seemed enthusiastic but the critics were muted. It was a disappointment.

For all of us at the Kennedy Center, the summer of 2002 will always be known as the "Sondheim summer." After all the preparatory work, we finally went into rehearsal for *Sweeney Todd* in April. The night before I hosted a party for the cast and designers in my home. We wanted to create a warm atmosphere so the artists felt safe to do their best work and to take risks. We also felt we had something to prove; since many of the performers were from New York, we wanted them to know we knew how to run a theater project even if we were new at it.

Those first few rehearsals were magical. To hear such talented people dive into their roles reminded us why we had been planning this for so long. The cast members were also incredibly nice. There was no temperament. Just talent. Steve attended the first rehearsal—it all seemed historic.

Each week another cast would arrive and we repeated the process. All the groups were different; all were talented. And all got into the rhythm of "Camp Sondheim." After rehearsals, and later, after performances, the actors would gather at the restaurant across the street and the casts could intermingle. The theater world is a small one, so many of the performers had worked together before.

Shortly after rehearsals began, we held the first event of the Sondheim Celebration, a symposium with Frank Rich interviewing Steve. Originally, we planned to hold this in the Terrace Theater, which seats five hundred. After all the press we received, we moved it to the Concert Hall and filled all twenty-four hundred seats. I made a short speech and was immensely gratified by the public's warm and enthusiastic greeting when I entered the stage. It was clear the public was thrilled that this project was about to begin.

Steven and Frank were perfect. They were funny and warm and informative and the audience roared with approval. It augured well for the rest of the festival. The tech week (technical rehearsals) for *Sweeney Todd* did not. We had only allowed a few days on the stage for each cast. (Typically a Broadway show will have several weeks to get the sets and lights and sound to work properly and to allow the cast to become familiar with the stage.) This was a decision we would all regret but was forced by financial concerns. Working in rep—with a different show each night—is extremely expensive. We had also developed the schedule when we had anticipated very simple sets. Although the set designs became more elaborate, we were stuck with the original rehearsal and performance schedule since tickets had already been sold.

The *Sweeney* set was complicated. Huge pieces of scenery were moved by stagehands and the actors. The lighting was complicated and the sound system tricky. (The sound never worked very well and was the weakest part of the festival.) The dress rehearsal on Friday afternoon (we opened that night) was a fiasco. At one point, Brian Stokes Mitchell almost fell ten feet to the floor as a staircase was not moved in time to the proper place. We all were petrified about the opening that night. We did not want our vaunted Sondheim Celebration to go down as a huge fiasco. We did not want the few people who questioned our ability to mount such a large project to be able to gloat.

But the theater gods smiled on us and it was one of those magical performances. The audience went wild from the first note and did not stop. Stokes and Christine were unbelievably good. The entire ensemble jelled perfectly. The curtain calls were as ecstatic as I have ever seen. Backstage we were all sobbing, including Steve. We had been so tense all week and yet we had produced a truly great show.

The reviews were ecstatic as well, except for the *Washington Post*, which was admiring but reserved. We were disappointed, but the avalanche of great reviews elsewhere made up for it. The *New York Times* raved.

The cast of *Company* watched the first performance of *Sweeney Todd* and was concerned that their show would not measure up. It was a stormy rehearsal period and the cast had not had the benefit of an audience to laugh at the extended book scenes; that is, long scenes with dialogue and no music. While *Company*'s tech week was not as harried as *Sweeney*'s the week before, everyone was nervous. Opening night was another triumph. The critics were even more enthusiastic. We were on a roll.

Sunday in the Park is my favorite Sondheim musical; Eric had devised an ingenious ending to the first act that took one's breath away; every audience applauded as his coup de théâtre was revealed. The first three shows ran in repertory while the second group was rehearsed. Our children's version of *Into the Woods* gave student performers a chance to take the stage; Steve cried at the opening. Mandy Patinkin and Barbara Cook gave us beautiful one-person shows; Barbara also led a master class that revealed why she is so admired.

By the time we opened our second set of shows, we were far more experienced. *Merrily* opened with unanimous praise for Raul's amazing performance of Charlie. Each night during the overture and before the curtain was raised, the entire cast went on stage and danced. We called it "the dance party." Even Steve joined in one night. *Merrily* was, for me, the surprise of the series. Eric's *Passion* was an astonishing accomplishment. It was the jewel of the series. And Blair Brown and John Dossett and Doug Sills and Randy Graf gave us a wonderful *Night Music*.

On the last night of *Night Music*, I asked the entire organization to join the curtain call: the stagehands who had worked so hard to mount so many shows, the ushers, the administrators. It was a joyful and sad moment. We were all so proud of the artistic accomplishment and the remarkable press we had received.

None of us wanted it to end and I decided to attempt a one-night compendium of our celebration in New York. Almost all of the principals made themselves available for what turned into a love-fest at Avery Fisher Hall. For us, it was a fitting reunion of Camp Sondheim.

Before, during, and after the celebration, the press was astonishing. From virtually every American city and many foreign cities, journalists covered our celebration. It helped attract audience members from all fifty states and thirty-eight foreign countries. I was trying to turn the Kennedy Center into a destination, but this was far more than I could have dreamed of. Virtually every critic named the Sondheim Celebration as one of the top ten theater events of the year and *Entertainment Weekly* named us as number one. Good art, well marketed, indeed.

The after-affects of the celebration are still being felt. It was clear that the Kennedy Center was no longer just a touring house, and it was equally clear that despite an economic recession, a major artistic project could flourish and could contribute to the organization. Contributions reached record levels in the face of a major stock market decline.

The impact on our staff was equally dramatic. There was pride that we had done something amazing. Even the stagehands union voted to give a twenty-five-thousand-dollar donation to the Kennedy Center after the celebration. They wanted to encourage us to do work like this again.

Sondheim was not all that was happening at the Center. The first entry in the Catherine B. Reynolds Foundation Series for Artistic Excellence was a remarkable evening that paired the Bolshoi Opera and the Bolshoi Ballet in a very rare joint performance. The performance was followed by a lavish dinner with a stellar guest list including three Supreme Court justices and a who's who of Washington. It was a fitting way to begin this fantastic series.

But we had no time to rest. September 2002 was the busiest month in our history. We mounted a concert to honor the first anniversary of September 11, we opened our first Prelude Festival, we received congressional authorization for the Plaza Project, we initiated our Capacity Building Program, and we welcomed our second class of Fellows. The September 11 concert was broadcast nationally on NBC with Tom Brokaw as host. President Bush, Mrs. Bush, and Caroline Kennedy Schlossberg appeared on the stage, and a host of talented performers and celebrities contributed their services, including Gloria Estefan, Plácido Domingo, Renée Fleming, Aretha Franklin, Rudolph Giuliani, Al Green, India. Arie, Chris Isaak, Alan Jackson, and Reba McEntire.

We also created a new festival called Prelude to open the season. I felt the year before that the Washington arts season just seemed to start without any fanfare, unlike the big openings in other cities. I wanted to do something special to mark the new season, and I wanted to focus on popular attractions that would draw many people to the arts. I also wanted to allow other D.C. area arts organizations to participate.

Prelude included NSO concerts; a play reading series (that included many local theater companies); the Washington National Opera; the Washington Ballet, dancing on the River Terrace; the Flying Karamazov Brothers; and a sing-along screening of *The Sound of Music*. Thousands of fans of the movie showed up in costume to sing along with the movie. It was a ridiculous and fun event. Our Open House event (during which every theater of the Center runs all day with special programming at no cost to the audience) formed the centerpiece of the festival. Thousands and thousands of people attended Prelude events and we all believed a new tradition had started.

As Prelude concluded, we received authorization from Congress for the Plaza Project. It had taken almost one full year to receive approval from the two relevant committees and the two Houses of Congress and to get the signature from President Bush. We had spent hundreds of hours lobbying for this piece of legislation, which authorized Congress to fund the Plaza Project and authorized us to raise money to pay for the two new buildings. The lobbying process is a complicated and mysterious one, and as a novice, I was especially frustrated. One talks and talks to members of Congress and hopes that the legislation will happen. Behind the scenes, the wonderful congressional staff members make the process work. We gave a special dinner to thank those staff members most involved with the project. I was given a copy of the legislation with one of the president's pens. It is a treasured souvenir of a mammoth effort.

Unfortunately, congressional authorization does not mean you get the cash. In January 2003 we announced the engagement of Rafael Viñoly as our architect of the Plaza Project. His appointment followed a ten-month search process during which we interviewed dozens of architects, flew to view buildings, reviewed references, and studied design concepts. The diverse search committee was unanimous in its decision to select Rafael.

His concept for the Plaza immediately made sense to everyone. He reduced the Plaza size, created a monumental fountain, extended our back porch over the Potomac, moved the buildings closer together, and did it all with a grace and style that attracted the committee, the public, and the press. The architecture critic for the *Post*, Ben Forgey, was enthusiastic in his praise, as were the leaders of the various agencies who had to approve the project: the Department of Transportation, the District of Columbia, the National Park Service, the Commission of Fine Arts, and the National Capital Planning Commission.

This project was always conceived of as a public/private partnership, and we knew we had to raise about $300 million in private funds to construct the two new buildings. After a brief negotiation, the Catherine B. Reynolds Foundation committed to providing $100 million to this project. We were overjoyed. Quickly another $50 million in pledges was identified. We grew very optimistic that we could raise the required private funds.

But as the time drew near for the writing of the National Highway Trust Fund legislation, it became clear that the public funds for all of the anticipated projects would not be available. The war in Iraq forced Congress to reduce this legislation by approximately $100 billion, and many projects, including our own, were eliminated. It was a sad day for us when we had to announce the end of the Plaza Project and offer the money pledged back to the donors. But I had an institution to run, and I had to reinvigorate my staff, board, donors and audience.

In this case it was not difficult to do. I have always believed that the important work of the Kennedy Center or any not-for-profit organization is not its facility but the programming it presents. And we had a great deal of programming to attend to.

For the second Catherine B. Reynolds Foundation Series for Artistic Excellence I wanted to do something very different from the Bolshoi but equally special. We discussed mounting a concert version of *Carmen Jones*, Oscar Hammerstein's re-work of Bizet's *Carmen*. It made great sense to me since we could showcase the National Symphony Orchestra and could entice many leading performers to fill the wonderful roles in that work.

The casting process quickly led to Vanessa Williams and Harolyn Blackwell, but we had a difficult time finding a tenor who could be believable and could sing the part. We heard about an African-American tenor who was working in England. On a trip there, I heard Tom Randle and was impressed. He helped complete the picture. Oscar de la Renta agreed to do the costumes, and I asked Plácido Domingo to conduct. With more than two hundred in the cast, it was a remarkable project and attracted a truly diverse audience to the Center.

While *Carmen Jones* was a very public success, I had a very private moment that ranks with the most exciting of my career: I was invited to have lunch with the Supreme Court. All of the justices. Justice Stephen Breyer, a music enthusiast, issued the invitation. I had already met Justices O'Connor, Ginsburg, Scalia, and Kennedy at Kennedy Center performances and events. But to sit down to lunch with all nine was astonishing. We discussed the challenges of running arts organizations, the impact of the economic decline, the way arts are funded in Europe, the future of the Kennedy Center, and a range of other arts-related issues. All nine justices were active participants and all were extremely gracious to this overwhelmed arts administrator. It placed in sharp relief the advantages of running a national cultural center.

From the intimacy of the Supreme Court I moved quickly to the blitzkrieg surrounding the twenty-fifth anniversary of the Kennedy Center Honors. We had a special group of honorees: Chita Rivera, James Levine, Elizabeth Taylor, James Earl Jones, and Paul Simon. I was especially pleased that James Levine accepted the award. He has always been a hero to me. The press, of course, focused on Ms. Taylor, who could not have been more charming during the entire awards weekend. Paul Simon was a replacement for Paul McCartney, who had accepted the honor and then had to decline because of a family wedding. We were obviously disappointed, but Paul Simon was a most deserving honoree in any event.

In the spring of 2003 we inaugurated a new relationship with the Royal Shakespeare Company. I had developed a strong friendship with the leadership of this organization while I ran the Royal Opera House and thought it would be a great complement to our theater programming. While the first presentation, *As You Like It*, was not stellar, future installments were superb, especially *The Taming of the Shrew* and *The Canterbury Tales*. (I experienced one of the funnier typos in my career during *As You Like It*. A computerized spell-checker at our program printers changed our acknowledgment of a deeply appreciated gift from the Prince of Wales Foundation to one from the Prince of Whales Foundation!)

In truth, the 2002/2003 theater season was a disappointment in every respect. Perhaps it was to be expected after the highs of the Sondheim Celebration, but both *Tell Me on a Sunday* and *Stones in His Pockets* were unsuccessful and a major touring production of *Oklahoma* was cancelled. We tried for months to find an acceptable alternative, and while Barbara Cook is a truly astonishing performer, she could not quite fill the gap created by this cancelled production. If we were going to transform the Kennedy Center into a true arts destination, I knew we had to become more consistent; we could not simply rest on our Sondheim laurels.

The following season did fare much better, though it began with a major disappointment. With the success of the Sondheim Celebration two seasons before, we were especially excited to be one of two presenters of a new Sondheim musical, *Bounce*. (In fact, the Kennedy Center had commissioned the first workshop of this work years earlier.) But this was clearly a work in formation, and neither the audience nor the critics were particularly kind. But the remainder of the 2003/2004 season included one highlight after another; every art form featured performances of the highest caliber and restored my faith in my programming acumen.

We staged a Tchaikovsky Festival that opened with the NSO and Leonard Slatkin with Yefim Bronfman, Gil Shaham, and Yo-Yo Ma in a single concert and included the Kirov Opera with Valery Gergiev, the

Kirov Ballet, the Suzanne Farrell Ballet, and the Vermeer String Quartet. This festival suggested the Center's ability to program across art forms, exactly the kind of curation I wanted to feature.

We mounted a French Festival that included a full slate of NSO performances, the American debut of L'Opéra Comique, several theater productions, Les Arts Florissants, Lyon Opera Ballet, and a series of jazz performances. Funding this festival was a challenge given the prevailing political climate between the United States and France, but I felt that holding the festival, after three years of planning, was essential to show that arts and politics cannot mix—even at the national cultural center.

Another innovation for that season was the introduction of our Conservatory Project. I wanted to focus on presenting the best young performers when they are still students. We arranged with great American conservatories (Juilliard, Curtis, Eastman, etc.) to present an evening of their best students, one night per conservatory. These performances took place in the intimate Terrace Theater but were part of the Center's Millennium Stage performances. Every day of the year, the Center presents a free performance at 6 P.M. These performances are also broadcast over the Internet. This remarkable series allows people with little knowledge of the arts, or little to spend, to experience the performing arts. (The entire Millennium Stage series was the idea of Jim Johnson and has created a whole new audience for the Center. During our AmericArtes festival, we had the pop star Juanes perform on the Millennium Stage; nine thousand young people arrived and screamed for an hour.)

This season also included the first appearances by the New York City Ballet since 1987. The City Ballet is obviously an American treasure. Unfortunately, the City Ballet's contract requires its own orchestra to play at all performances, at home or on tour. And the Kennedy Center's contract requires the use of its own Opera House Orchestra at all ballet performances. We solved that problem in 2002 by persuading both orchestras to agree to sharing the work; our orchestra plays one year, theirs the next. This was a simple solution to a problem that kept a premier organization out of Washington. The first engagement, in March 2004, featured the works of George Balanchine, the founder of the City Ballet, in his 100th anniversary year.

This great season ended with our Tennessee Williams Festival, which included new productions of *A Streetcar Named Desire*, *Cat on a Hot Tin*

Roof, and *The Glass Menagerie.* I wanted to mount these works to remind our audience of the beauty of the language of this great American play-wright. I think we were successful. *Streetcar* and *Cat* were both generally strong productions. I will never forget George Grizzard's soulful and sad interpretation of Big Daddy, and Amy Ryan was a remarkable Stella. We had originally announced *Night of the Iguana* instead of *Menagerie,* but tragically, the director, Gerald Gutierrez, passed away before rehears-als began and our replacement, Greg Mosher, wanted to do *Menagerie* instead. But *The Glass Menagerie* was perfect; along with our production of *Passion* two years earlier, and *Der Rosenkavalier* at the Royal Opera House, *Menagerie* was one of the most important productions of my ca-reer. Sally Field and Jason Butler Harner headed a cast that could not be topped. Indeed, our three Williams productions received better reviews than the same three plays in concurrent Broadway productions, a source of great pride for all of us.

We opened the Williams Festival with a special interview with four great actresses — Zoe Caldwell, Rosemary Harris, Estelle Parsons, and Eva Marie Saint — all of whom had worked with Williams. We also in-cluded a series of one-act plays produced by the Shakespeare Theatre Company named *Five by Tenn.* These were great ways to build interest among the audience and the press and made the festival "larger" than it would otherwise have been. Adding elements to a core project has always been one of my "tricks" for attracting more press attention; these new elements also provide additional underwriting opportunities.

It is difficult to describe adequately the variety of issues and tasks one manages as president of the Kennedy Center. In addition to develop-ing and implementing performances and education programs, one is also responsible for maintaining a large facility, ensuring fiscal health, raising substantial amounts of funds, selling large numbers of tickets, managing a large staff, and working with Congress. Perhaps that is why I have stayed interested for so many years!

The 2003/2004 season set an incredibly high bar that we tried to reach in future seasons. The following season included one of my favor-ite projects: Masters of African-American Choreography. Since my time at Ailey, I have been fascinated by the evolution of African-American modern dance during the twentieth century. The works migrated from Afro-Caribbean movement to social protest to postmodern. I felt it was important to recognize this development and to honor those choreographers who were so influential in this evolution.

We mounted a one-week festival that featured more than fifteen African-American modern dance companies. Each night focused on a particular theme; taken together, they traced an amazing history. Opening night was spectacular. We hosted a dinner for approximately thirty dance legends (unfortunately Katherine Dunham was ill and could not make it from the hotel to the Center) who were truly excited and surprised by the attention they received. During the performance, I called each to the stage. The audience responded with ever-increasing roars of approval and esteem. No one who was there that night will forget it.

That season also included a long (perhaps too long) festival of American arts from the 1940s. We had wanted to mount a festival of American works and it was Leonard Slatkin who came up with the idea of limiting it to the 1940s—a decade of amazing artistic accomplishment and excitement in this country. We featured symphonic music by Bernstein and Copland, screened the major movies of the 1940s, had a series of jazz performances, hosted both the New York City Ballet and ABT (both of which were formed in the 1940s), and mounted a new production of *Mr. Roberts*. We learned that festivals that are too long (this one lasted from January to June) do not maintain the interest of the public and the press, but we were pleased with the theme and its execution, with one major exception. We had decided to mount a semi-staged version of Blitzstein's work *Regina*. We made the (honest) mistake of putting the work on our theater subscription; this work had originally been produced on Broadway. But it really is an opera and our theater subscribers howled.

We also inaugurated a series, Voices of the Arts, that allowed me to interview some of the most important arts personalities. The series, which ran for two years, included interviews with Marilyn Horne, John Lithgow, Hal Prince, Susan Stroman, and Christine Baranski. For me, the highlight was an interview with James Conlon, who spoke eloquently about the effect of the Holocaust on the direction of classical music. This series allowed us to experiment with pod-casting, one of the new technologies that are making it easier for us to market and disseminate arts and education.

Another new venture for the Kennedy Center was the Suzanne Farrell Ballet, which emerged from a summer program this great American ballerina created at the Kennedy Center. What makes this project so exciting is that Suzanne is committed to recreating "lost" Balanchine ballets. In June 2005 Suzanne recreated Mr. Balanchine's full-length ballet *Don Quixote*, a huge accomplishment.

The 2005/2006 season was another season of highlights. It was the seventy-fifth anniversary of the National Symphony Orchestra, and we had the opportunity to celebrate the progress we had made in grand style, opening with our NSO Ball featuring Emanuel Ax, Yo-Yo Ma, and Itzhak Perlman in the Beethoven *Triple Concerto* and ending with Mahler's *Eighth Symphony*, the *Symphony of a Thousand*, which I had sung at Tanglewood thirty-five years before.

But the season also included an astonishing Festival of China, which featured some nine hundred performers from that country in numerous art forms: puppet theater, modern dance, drumming, ballet, symphonic music, popular music. Every performance sold out. The Festival started with a mixed program followed by fireworks designed by a major Chinese "explosion artist." Our guests stood on the roof of the Center and enjoyed amazing, and amazingly loud, fireworks. All proper authorities had been notified, as had the news media. Thousands of people lined the bridges and enjoyed the show. But many people living near the Center were not expecting fireworks on October 1 and were frightened by the loud booms. We set the record for 911 calls that evening. One irate gentleman wrote to the *Washington Post* that "his children no longer had only Osama bin Laden to fear but the Kennedy Center as well!" That seemed a bit of overkill. The logistics of this festival, from obtaining visas to organizing food and lodging for nine hundred artists, defied the imagination. But I believed it was important to expose Americans to the art from this nation that was becoming so important in virtually every sector of our lives.

I tried a new venture in 2006—a Festival of Country Music. I love country music and believed that it was time for an arts center to treat this music seriously. Once again, every performance was sold out. A highlight for me was a Millennium Stage performance by Earl Scruggs and his family: a living legend playing for thousands and thousands of happy fans. Using the Millennium Stage as an integral part of our festivals has been a priority for me; it truly fulfills our desire to offer the best in art to everyone.

One of the challenges of running a comprehensive arts center is to find new ways to put a spotlight on new works. When I arrived at the Kennedy Center, we sponsored a program called the Fund for New America Plays. We gave small grants to many theaters to produce selected new works by American playwrights. I felt that the grants were so small that they had become somewhat gratuitous and few of the plays were ever performed at the Center. We looked for a new approach for the same mission: to encourage important new American plays. In 2006 we launched the new version of the Fund for New American Plays: we gave the entire grant to one regional theater company and guaranteed to stage that play at the Kennedy Center after its initial run. To date the results have not been very satisfying.

Another challenge we face is finding new ways to showcase particular art forms. This is especially true for ballet. We have developed an amazing ballet series, but the number of standard repertory works is small, so repetition is common. We developed an idea for presenting ballet students from the best ballet schools in the world. While ballet companies have started to look more and more alike as dancers and repertory cross boundaries, training is still different country by country. We created a series of performances with students from the Mariinsky (Kirov) School, Paris Opera Ballet School, Royal Ballet School, New National Theater of Japan School, and Dance Theatre of Harlem. I was excited about these performances though no one else seemed to care, until the day of the performances. Our audiences were entranced and the critics were thrilled, so much so that we are repeating the program every two years into the future. This confirmed my belief that arts organizations have their greatest success when they have the courage to take the lead and do something different.

Perhaps the most important event of that season was the opening of our Family Theater. For decades, the Kennedy Center hosted the American Film Institute (AFI) in a black box type space with bleachers and car parts on the wall (go figure). When the AFI decided to build its own facility, we decided to build a proper theater to focus on our work for children and family audiences. This new theater with 320 seats has become a hive of activity and a central part of our education activities.

And the season closed with our own production of *Mame*. We asked Christine Baranski, who had been so wonderful in *Sweeney Todd*, to take the title role. Eric Schaeffer directed a fabulous production that had the audiences cheering from beginning to end. We had hopes of taking this production to Broadway, but our production was so large that no Broadway producer could afford it. And that is the way it should be. Not-for-profit arts organizations should be doing work that commercial producers won't consider either because the work is too large (*Mame*) or too risky (Sondheim). This is what justifies the use of tax-deductible contributions.

Like the 2002/2003 season, the 2005/2006 season was a landmark that convinced me that we were on the right track with our programming and that we were truly changing the nature of the national cultural center.

Shortly after I arrived at the Kennedy Center, I hosted a breakfast for local arts leaders. It was clear that the Center had not developed strong relationships with our sister arts organizations and was viewed as an unfriendly behemoth. We rectified this in part by hosting several local theater companies as they built new facilities, utilizing many local choruses in NSO performances, hosting our play reading program during Prelude, including a program by the Shakespeare Theatre Company during the Tennessee Williams events, and having such a close relationship with Eric Schaeffer. But I wanted a large project to indicate the strength and camaraderie of local arts organizations. I approached Michael Kahn, head of the Shakespeare Theatre Company, about creating a D.C.-wide Shakespeare Festival. No artist has inspired the work of so many other art forms as Shakespeare. I felt we could involve dozens of local groups. Michael was excited by the idea and agreed to curate the festival.

The Shakespeare in Washington Festival turned out to be a major success for the more than sixty arts organizations that participated. We worked with the Shakespeare Theatre to develop marketing materials and web sites and to coordinate with the Convention and Tourism Board. But each organization was responsible for its own budget, fund-raising and expenses; this allowed the festival to proceed without friction.

We decided to open the festival with a free reading of *Twelfth Night* on Twelfth Night. There was so much publicity for the new festival that seventy-two hundred people showed up for the twenty-four hundred seats in our Concert Hall. And this was for the reading of a Shakespeare play! We included the Kirov Opera and Ballet, ABT, New York City Ballet, and Royal Shakespeare Company (in the fifth and last installment of our agreement), among other programming in our part of the Shakespeare project.

Shortly after we opened the Shakespeare in Washington Festival we celebrated the tenth anniversary of the Millennium Stage with events in our three big theaters—the NSO in the Concert Hall, Alvin Ailey in the Eisenhower Theater, and indie-rocker Sufjan Stevens in the Opera House. The lines for the rock performance started to form twenty-four hours before the ticket giveaway. We believed that the three different programs demonstrated the variety of Millennium Stage offerings and the diversity of the Kennedy Center.

The next month saw the major jazz program of my tenure: Jazz in Our Times. The week-long festival was highlighted by an astonishing evening featuring thirty-five of the greatest living jazz musicians—from Dave Brubeck to Wynton Marsalis, Nancy Wilson to Cleo Laine. The audience could not believe the embarrassment of riches.

A less happy event was our production of *Carnival*. *Carnival* is a lovely small musical that features a beautiful score and a delicate plot. I did not agree with the director's choices from the start. He saw it as a dramatic story with music; I saw it as a beautiful score with a deceptively simple story line. As discussions progressed, I was increasingly unhappy about many planned elements of the production, but I felt I had to let the director pursue his vision. In the end, the show enjoyed modest critical and audience support, but I remained unhappy.

I am hoping for more success with our planned festival of the works of August Wilson in the 2007/2008 season. We will also host a major festival of Japan, a festival of a cappella music (a particular favorite of mine), the second installment of our Protégés project, a new cabaret series curated by Barbara Cook, a concert version of *Eugene Onegin* by the NSO, productions of *Otello* and *Pique Dame* by the Kirov Opera, a major project by Shen Wei Dance Arts (our new resident modern dance organization), and on and on. A typical season at the Kennedy Center.

It is virtually impossible to list all of the programming at the Kennedy Center in one season. We offer a total of two thousand performances, half of which we present, the remainder of which are presented by others.

While this programming is the public face of the Kennedy Center, we coincidentally produce the nation's largest performing arts education program. This is where the name *national cultural center* is manifested. We work with talented young performers, take arts into the classroom, and tour children's productions to all fifty states. When I arrived at the Center, we offered a host of disparate programs that I have attempted to rationalize. The centerpiece of our education programming is our work in the classroom. As more and more public school systems have eliminated arts funding, we and other arts organizations have jumped in to fill the breach. We offer teacher training, web sites, satellite systems, and numerous other programs to put arts in the classroom in every state. I have focused on supporting those programs that are truly scalable—where we can use our size and resources to make real change on a national level. Our ArtsEdge web site, for example, provides materials to teachers wanting to present arts in their classrooms and provides online activities for children. We have increased the size of this program dramatically since it can reach teachers and students in every region of the globe. In fact, there are new modules on ArtsEdge for every Kennedy Center festival. We also merged with another international arts organization, VSA arts, which provides arts education and programming for people who have disabilities.

Although every arts education program sounds wonderful, I have grown increasingly frustrated with the way we teach arts in the schools. While many students enjoy many arts experiences, the learning is virtually always episodic. Those children with teachers who love the arts might have many arts exposures in one year. But if their next teachers do not like the arts, they may have none. We teach no other subject in this haphazard manner. Darrell Ayers, the head of our education program, and I have been working on a new approach to unite the resources of the Kennedy Center, a given local community, and its school system to create a systematic approach to arts education. We are about to test market this approach in several U.S. communities. We were given extra ammunition for our efforts when an independent research center determined that our program of arts education did the most to raise children's reading and math scores in a test of schools in Maryland.

The newest element of our education practice is the one I introduced when we opened our Kennedy Center Arts Management Institute. (We quietly changed the name from Vilar Arts Management Institute when Mr. Vilar suffered his well-publicized financial challenges.) The Fellows program instituted in 2001 continues to this day. To date, sixty-six Fellows have graduated from our program and occupy senior roles at arts organizations throughout the world. In 2006 we hosted a five-year reunion for graduate Fellows. About half of our Fellows returned and discussed the progress they were making in their organizations. It was a very proud moment for all of us who had spent time training these talented young people.

But our arts management programming has grown far beyond the Institute. Our Capacity Building Program is one of the most significant new programs we have launched at the Kennedy Center both in its own right and because of the additional programs it spawned.

Through my work at Ailey and various consulting assignments, I had grown increasingly concerned about the fate of America's African-American, Latino, Asian-American, and Native American arts organizations since only three have budgets of more than $3 million. Too many hang by a thread and are threatened with closure almost daily. I believed if the Kennedy Center is to be *the* national cultural center, we must assist smaller arts organizations, and if we are to have a healthy arts ecology, we needed all kinds of organizations to thrive.

I thought that the Kennedy Center could play a role in training the leaders of these arts organizations. We began with a symposium at Yale University in early 2002. Several minority theater executives joined together to discuss methods for improving fund-raising, board productivity, and marketing. After the seminar concluded, the groups were unanimous in asking for additional help. I thought about this all summer and devised the Capacity Building Program. We selected a group of seventeen arts organizations from Washington, New York, Los Angeles, Dayton, Philadelphia, and other cities to participate.

Every few weeks I would enter an online chat room with the leaders of these arts organizations to discuss a particular subject: building an individual donor base, institutional marketing, soliciting new board members, and so forth. These online sessions gave everyone a chance to ask questions and share experiences. Once a year, everyone gathered at the Kennedy Center for a three-day symposium. These were some of the most stimulating days in my career. We have added many new groups to the original seventeen and continue this rewarding program to this day.

This program evolved into additional programs for arts organizations in New York City, for mid-sized orchestras, and, most recently, for arts organization in the Washington, D.C., area. We also instituted a training program for board members. We found that if we simply worked with staff members we were not fully addressing the challenges of most arts organizations. Little training was available for members of performing arts boards; they join boards filled with excitement and generosity but without the knowledge they need to be fully effective. Our three-day board programs are now some of our most popular.

In a few instances we worked in a focused way with organizations in trouble. I played a central role in bringing the Dance Theatre of Harlem organization back to life after it closed its doors. After Hurricane Katrina we adopted the Louisiana Philharmonic Orchestra. I have taken six trips to New Orleans since the devastating storm and have worked to raise money, train staff and board, and work on strategic planning for that remarkable organization.

Beginning with an invitation by the United States Department of State to teach in Mexico, we have begun to build an international practice as well. For the past four years we have worked to help small and mid-sized arts organizations in Mexico to raise more funds and to sell more tickets. We have also worked to help the government change arts funding practices to encourage this entrepreneurial behavior. In recognition of my work there, the Mexican government awarded me the Order of the Aztec Eagle, their highest honor for foreigners.

As we were preparing for our China Festival in 2006, we were approached by the Chinese government about instituting arts management training in that country. To date, we have taught hundreds of Chinese arts managers and students in China and in Washington. Our work in China inspired our new approach to cultural exchange: we import art from countries and return expertise in arts management. Americans have learned more sophisticated marketing and fund-raising techniques since we do not enjoy the high levels of central government support available in almost every other country.

Our work internationally has grown to include Pakistan and the twenty-two Arab countries and will shortly include Central Europe, France, South Africa, South America, and Southeast Asia. Our work in the Arab countries began with a trip to Baghdad in 2003 during which

I negotiated a tour to Washington by the Iraq National Symphony. This trip was truly memorable; I had never toured a country at war. I flew into Iraq with a group of State Department officials; in midair the fuel line snapped on our C-130 airplane and we were instructed to "run for our lives" when the plane landed. We obeyed. We flew around the city in Blackhawk helicopters and traveled with tank convoys. It was sad and sobering but inspirational as well. In the midst of this environment we heard a rehearsal by the symphony and a chamber music concert, viewed ancient and contemporary art, and developed firsthand knowledge of the distinguished cultural history of the country.

Hosting the orchestra in Washington was a joy, and their performance with members of the NSO was very moving. The most common refrain I heard was "I did not know Iraq had a symphony." Americans know very little about other people; we read a great deal about international politics but little about the people who live in these countries. That is why introducing art from abroad is so crucial at this time. Helen Henderson, a remarkable philanthropist and Kennedy Center Trustee, has supported this work in every way possible.

Conversely, our teaching abroad helps create the impression of Americans as knowledgeable and generous people. Some people have suggested that we should simply export American artists abroad, but I have learned from my work in England, South Africa, and elsewhere, that most people around the world believe they experience enough American culture, via movies, television, and popular music. Our offer to help their local cultures survive and thrive is considered a far more generous act. Nowhere was this more evident than during our seminar in Cairo in March 2007, when 140 Arab arts leaders from seventeen Arab nations gathered to hear me teach for three days. These were honest, challenging, and rewarding sessions; politics was rarely mentioned.

All of this work was completed by an astonishing staff and a dedicated board. In 2002, Jim Johnson announced that he would step down as chairman in early 2004. While the news was not unexpected since Jim served for eight years, it was still a blow. Jim had a historic impact on the Center. He professionalized management, built the fund-raising effort, and, most important, created the Millennium Stage.

After an exhaustive search process, the board elected Stephen A. Schwarzman as chairman. Steve has been a different kind of chairman from Jim. Steve has been an incredible fund-raiser for the Center and has very generously underwritten our theater programming. Steve lives in New York and plays less of a hands-on role than Jim did. This seems a natural evolution. When the Center was opened, one man, Roger Stevens, was both chairman and president. Over the past thirty-six years the roles of leadership have evolved. Today the president runs the center with the board and its chair providing oversight. It is a model that works at this point in time.

I am less convinced that the governance structure is effective. Our board is made up of thirty-six presidential appointees, fourteen members of Congress, three cabinet secretaries, and six ex-officio members. This means that our board changes its profile very frequently and allows for little institutional memory. This, in turn, gives the staff a bit too much authority. If they handle this authority well, matters run smoothly. But I worry about the alternative.

Attending to evolution in board and staff is a central part of the leader's role. One important position that is currently in transition is music director of the National Symphony Orchestra. While Leonard Slatkin was one of the first people I met when I was considering joining the Kennedy Center, we have traveled a bumpy road. It became clear to both of us that it was time for him to leave the NSO and 2007/2008 will be his last season. Leonard has done a great deal to build the quality of the orchestra over more than a decade; we are forever in his debt. Selecting a new music director is a central challenge for the remainder of my tenure at the Kennedy Center. This task is made much simpler given the extraordinary generosity of Roger and Vicki Sant, who endowed the music director's position.

A second major transition that I am currently preparing for is my own departure from the Center at the end of 2011. I will have run the Kennedy Center for eleven years; I think it is essential to change leadership of a presenting organization every decade so that the audience can enjoy different perspectives and aesthetics.

While the Kennedy Center was not a classic turnaround story, I have learned that every arts organization faces challenges, and therefore leading any arts organization requires change. The Kennedy Center needed an artistic and image turnaround, and I feel confident that we will have made great progress toward these ends by the time I leave. We have created a much deeper and more exciting program of arts and education, we have become a true player on the international arts scene, and we have developed into the cultural destination I envisioned in 2000.

We have also refurbished most of our building. We have completely renovated all three of the main theaters. We restored the Grand Foyer, the shops, and both restaurants, and we expanded the garage and remodeled the entire outside environment. We installed substantial new security systems and entire new life safety systems. While managing these changes was challenging, especially under the watchful eye of the federal government, we have created a "new" Kennedy Center that far better serves the needs of a very diverse community. A particular focus of our renovation efforts has been to improve accessibility at the Center for people who have disabilities.

And, as theory would tell you, when you do good art and market it well, you will have the funds to support your art; we have had a surplus every year of my tenure. This is certainly not the central measure of success but an indication that the institution can pursue its mission safely into the decades ahead—the true goal of any arts administrator.

I have spent more time at the Kennedy Center than I have at any other institution, perhaps because I had artistic and educational as well as administrative responsibilities. Even though I still have four more years until I leave this job at the end of 2011, I am asked daily what I will do next. Will I go run another troubled institution? Will I teach in a university? Will I focus on international diplomacy? Will I work for a funding agency? The truthful answer is that I don't know. But as George says at the end of *Sunday in the Park*, "So many possibilities . . ."

CONCLUSION

When I started working in the arts, I did not know how to do a turnaround. The experiences at the Kansas City Ballet were clearly hit-or-miss. But I did know how to observe and analyze and I have always been painfully honest, especially about my own failures. The "most important 52 feet campaign" at the Kansas City Ballet was a mistake. But it taught me a great deal. In a turnaround you cannot make mistakes. And you must attend to the very short-term cash from ticket sales and small contributions. But the concept of institutional marketing was really born with that failed "52 feet" campaign. It was not *enough* to sell tickets because ticket sales will never balance a budget, let alone earn enough extra to achieve a turnaround.

And that is the cruel truth of a turnaround: simply breaking even is not good enough. Virtually every not-for-profit would be very happy to break even on a cash basis every year of its existence. But for the troubled arts organization, that is not good enough. Ironically, the sicker the organization, the more it needs to do better than break even to get healthy again. The Kansas City Ballet only needed to have a surplus of $125,000 to get back to ground zero. But the Royal Opera House needed $30 million to get whole!

Despite the differences in the size of the problem, it is important to note from every case study that the turnarounds took from one to three years for each organization. This is not an accident. Turnarounds must be accomplished in relatively short order. They cannot be extended for decades because it is difficult if not impossible to maintain the positive energy of the board, staff, donors, and volunteers for that long. And the truth is that no arts organization can get into a big enough hole that it should take more than a few years to fix. No one will lend enough money to any arts organization to allow them to get into a hole that takes decades to escape.

I wish it were that simple. In fact, the turnaround is not only about filling a deficit hole. Many organizations have received a few extraordinary gifts to fill a deficit and then fallen right back into the hole. The turnaround is about creating a sustainable organization, a well-functioning economic engine.

I have tried to do this with each organization I have managed. And with a few twists and turns, each of the organizations described in this book continues to prosper. But no arts organization is ever "safe" because the cushion is always so small. And I have found that every arts organization grows to the point that it becomes slightly uncomfortable because the dreams of artists almost always exceed current budget size.

That is why I include the Kennedy Center case. This is an organization that did not face life-or-death decisions and was not threatened by bankruptcy. I said upon my arrival that having run sick organizations for so long I now had a sense about how to run a healthy one. And that was not a joke. The strategies for fixing a sick organization are not much different from those that keep a healthy organization healthy.

It all starts and ends with a focus on programming. There is no reason for an arts organization to exist unless it does important programming. I begin and end every day worrying about the quality of the programming offered by my organizations because this is the key strategic variable.

But programming alone is not enough to ensure that an arts organization will prosper. This is why a comprehensive plan is required. To be honest, when I started my career I was convinced that the planning process had to result in a structured report. I am less certain of that today. I would rather create a short, clear, smart, entrepreneurial plan that can adapt to change quickly than a beautiful, long, well-reasoned leather-bound volume. In fact, best of all is a staff and board who think strategically every minute of the day.

If I have been successful it is because I enter every organization with a very clear idea of what I want to accomplish: how I plan to build an organization that will support excellent programming.

I waste no time developing these ideas and testing them with new colleagues and board members. The willingness to place this stake in the ground provides the kind of leadership that troubled organizations are thirsting for. More than anything else, people associated with a sick organization want someone to provide hope, to offer solutions, to move the organization.

This is the essence of turnaround leadership. Anyone with the chutz-pah to say here is where we are and here is where we are going and here is how we are going to get there, and is able to implement this plan with minimal risk and maximal return, can easily become a turnaround king.

INDEX OF NAMES